AMERICAN TROUBLEMAKERS

Cesar Chavez: Farm Worker Activist

AMERICAN TROUBLEMAKERS

Titles in Series

American TROUBLEMAKERS

CESAR CHAVEZ:
Farm Worker Activist

Burnham Holmes

With an Introduction by James P. Shenton

RSVP
RAINTREE STECK-VAUGHN
P U B L I S H E R S
The Steck-Vaughn Company

Austin, Texas

For Louis Phillips

CONSULTANTS

Yolanda Quintanilla-Finley
Teacher and Project Specialist
Corona Unified School District
Corona, California

Rudy Rodríguez
Professor and Chairperson
  Department of Reading
  and Bilingual Education
Texas Woman's University
Denton, Texas

MANAGING EDITOR
Richard G. Gallin

PROJECT MANAGER
Julie Klaus

PHOTO EDITOR
Margie Foster

A Gallin House Press Book

Library of Congress Cataloging-in-Publication Data
Holmes, Burnham, 1942-
    Cesar Chavez: Farm Worker Activist/ written by Burnham Holmes
       p.   cm. — (American troublemakers)
    "A Gallin House Press Book."
    Includes bibliographical references and index.
    Summary: A biography of the Mexican-American labor activist who helped organize the migrant farm workers and establish a union to fight for their rights.
    ISBN 0-8114-2326-3
    1. Chavez, Cesar, 1927-1993 — Juvenile literature.   2. Labor leaders — United States — Biography — Juvenile literature.   3. Strikes and lockouts — Agricultural laborers — California — Juvenile literature.   4. National Farm Workers Association —Juvenile literature. 5. United Farm Workers Organization Committee — Juvenile literature. [1. Chavez, Cesar, 1927- . 2. Labor leaders. 3. Mexican Americans — Biography. 4. United Farm Workers — History. 5. Migrant labor.]   I.Title.   II. Series.
HD6509.C48H65   1994
331.88'13'092—dc20
[B]
                            92-18225
                                CIP
                                  AC

Printed and bound in the United States.
1 2 3 4 5 6 7 8 9 0 LB 98 97 96 95 94 93

CONTENTS

Map

Cesar Chavez

INTRODUCTION

by James P. Shenton

Biography is the history of the individual lives of men and women. In all lives, there is a sequence that begins with birth, evolves into the development of character in childhood and adolescence, is followed by the emergence of maturity in adulthood, and finally concludes with death. All lives follow this pattern, although with each emerge the differences that make each life unique. These distinctive characteristics are usually determined by the particular area in which a person has been most active. An artist draws his or her specific identity from the area of the arts in which he or she has been most active. So the writer becomes an author; the musician, a performer or composer; the politician, a senator, governor, president, or statesperson. The intellectual discipline to which one is attached identifies the scientist, historian, economist, literary critic, or political scientist, among many. Some aspects of human behavior are identified as heroic, cowardly, corrupt, or just ordinary. The task of the biographer is to explain why a particular life is worth remembering. And if the effort is successful, the reader draws from it insights into a vast range of behavior patterns. In a sense, biography provides lessons from life.

Some lives become important because of the position a person holds. Typical would be that of a U.S. President in which a biographer compares the various incumbents to determine their comparative importance. Without question, Abraham Lincoln was a profoundly significant President, much more so than Warren G. Harding whose administration was swamped by corruption. Others achieve importance because of their role in a particular area. So Emily Dickinson and Carl Sandburg are recognized as important poets and Albert Einstein as a great scientist.

Implicit in the choice of biographical subjects is the idea that each somehow affected history. Their lives explain something about the world in which they lived, even as they affect our lives and those of generations to come. But there is another consideration: Some lives are more interesting than others. Within each life is a great story that illuminates human behavior.

7

Then there are those people who are troublemakers, people whom we cannot ignore. They are the people who both upset and fascinate us. Their singular quality is that they are uniquely different. Troublemakers are irritating, perhaps frightening, frustrating, and disturbing, but never dull. They march to their own drummer, and they are original.

One of the more remarkable things about the United States is how unpromising environments produce leaders who change American life. A good example is Cesar Chavez. He was born in 1927 to a Mexican-American family who farmed the hardscrabble desert near Yuma, Arizona. It was a difficult life but bearable until they lost their land during the Great Depression. The family turned to the life of migrant farm workers. They moved from place to place in California, harvesting the crops of fruits and vegetables, eking out a bare subsistence.

The lives of migrant farm workers provided experiences that shaped his outlook. Earning a meager few hundred dollars for a year's work as a family seared his memory. The poor, he learned, were powerless. Surrounded by food production, migrants often knew gnawing hunger. Outright racial attacks questioned their humanity. These experiences propelled Chavez into recognizing that only organization and protest would alter migrant farm workers' lives. Married after serving in the U.S. Navy during World War II, he returned to the familiar migrant routine. Unwilling to turn his back on the ways of living that had shaped him, Cesar Chavez committed his life to making a better world for the migrants. To achieve this result, he went to work as a union organizer. His tenacity was combined with a shrewd awareness that success depended on consumers supporting the effort.

The alliance between grape pickers and consumers was cemented by grape boycotts. It was a new departure in union organizing. To focus on the moral implications of the struggle, Chavez decided to fast. It reminded Americans that at the heart of the migrant farm workers' struggle was the need for decent lives based on adequate incomes. Throughout, he rejected appeals to violence. Chavez understood that change comes with struggle. But struggle can be peaceful. The nonviolent troublemaker can change the world. This is the gift of Cesar Chavez.

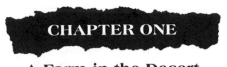

CHAPTER ONE

A Farm in the Desert

On October 15, 1966, a group of farm workers was striking alongside the road outside the entrance to a vineyard in Delano, California. The workers wanted the owner of the vineyard to employ workers who belonged to their union. The strikers believed that a union would provide farm workers with better pay, better working conditions, and better benefits, as well as more job security.

Unions have brought benefits not only to their own members. They have also struggled to make conditions better for many other workers in the United States. Over the years, unions have worked for and won for many workers the 8-hour workday, the 40-hour workweek, minimum wage laws, cost-of-living pay increases, and paid holidays and vacations. In addition, unions have gained for many workers two of the most valuable assets of any full-time job—medical insurance and pension plans.

But throughout much of this century, there has been one large group of people that has not profited from most of these gains. This group is made up of farm workers.

In 1935, Congress passed and President Franklin D. Roosevelt signed the National Labor Relations Act (the Wagner Act). This important law upheld the right of workers to join labor unions. It gave these unions the right to bargain collectively for the rights of their members. It defined unfair labor practices that some businesses practiced. Under this law, a National Labor Relations Board (NLRB) was set up to make sure that elections held by workers to choose unions were fair. The NLRB also could gather information about unfair employer practices and order such practices to stop.

Excluded from this right of collective bargaining and forming unions, however, were those people who worked in agribusiness. Agribusiness is the business of agriculture. Agribusiness includes more than just farming; it is the growing, picking, processing, packing, and storing of agricultural products.

Three decades after Congress had passed the National Labor Relations Act, farm workers were still struggling to gain basic workers' rights. That's why strikers had gathered along the entrance to the vineyard.

All of a sudden, a pickup truck sped down the road directly toward the group of strikers. One of the strikers, Manuel Rivera, was unable to get out of the way in time. The pickup slammed into the gray-haired man, knocking him to the ground. The pickup slowed to a standstill in a nearby ditch. Some of the strikers gathered around the fallen farm worker. Others moved toward the driver still sitting in the pickup.

Cesar Chavez first saw to it that help was on the way for Rivera. Then he made his way toward the driver. Chavez wanted to protect the driver from harm by the angry workers.

At five feet six inches tall and with a medium build, Cesar Chavez did not command attention because of his size. Chavez also did not look any different from most of the farm workers in his union. His hair was straight and black. Cesar Chavez's face echoed a Mexican-Indian heritage. He wore dusty work pants and a plaid shirt.

How Chavez really stood out was not in his physical appearance but in the strength of his beliefs. And one of his most basic beliefs was the one in action at that moment. This was his belief in the importance of nonviolence.

"I've learned that, if any movement is on the move, violence is the last thing wanted," Chavez once said. "Violence only seems necessary when people are desperate; frustration often leads to violence."

Frustration about low pay and poor working conditions has long been part of the lives of workers in agribusiness. Money is yanked out of the ground by migrant farm workers at a speed that would have made the heads of the prospectors spin during the gold rush days. Today this green gold has grown into a multi-billion-dollar-a-year enterprise. But in spite of all this prosperity, the migrant worker is still bent over mile-long rows of crops, barely scratching out a living.

Cesar Chavez spent his life working to change this injustice. He was the number one troublemaker for United States agribusiness. This is his story. It starts out in Mexico; his legacy continues to this day.

In the 1880s, Cesar Chavez's grandfather, known as Papa Chayo, escaped from Hacienda el Carmen in Chihuahua, Mexico. (A hacienda was a large plantation that often used forced labor to pick the grapes.) Crossing the border into the United States at El Paso, Texas, Papa Chayo found work on a railroad and in the fields. As soon as he could, he sent for his wife and their 14 children. In 1888, the Chavez family crossed the border from Mexico

Cesar Chavez's grandparents built this house in the North Gila Valley in what was then the Arizona Territory.

into the United States. Librado, Cesar Chavez's father, was only two years old at the time.

Papa Chayo later began a hauling business near Yuma in the Arizona Territory. Librado, who grew up to be a strapping man six feet tall and over 200 pounds, helped him. They hitched together long lines of mules and horses to pull the carts. In time they won a contract to haul firewood to the site of a federal dam being built in the desert. Five years later, Laguna Dam on the Colorado River was finished.

Papa Chayo and his wife, Dorotea (known as Mama Tella), liked the North Gila Valley wedged in between Mexico and California. They admired the rugged landscape of wide valleys flanked by mountains. They decided to set up a farm in the area. Under the Homestead Act of 1862, the federal government promised to give 160 acres to each head of a family who wanted to settle in remote regions of the country. The land would become the settler's land after five years of living on it. Near a canal, the family built an adobe house with two-foot-thick walls and a one-foot-thick roof. Then they dug ditches to carry water to future crops. They worked hard to turn their sandy soil and sagebrush into land suitable for farming. The year was 1909. Three years later the Arizona Territory became the state of Arizona, the 48th state in the Union.

Librado remained at the family farm until his marriage. In 1924, 38-year-old Librado married 32-year-old Juana Estrada. His bride was slender and barely five feet tall with shoulder-length black hair. A year later they became the happy parents of a girl whom they named Rita.

Two years later, on March 31, 1927, Juana Chavez gave birth to a son. They called the son Cesario Estrada Chavez. He was named Cesario (Papa Chayo's real name), after his grandfather, and Estrada after his mother. But as a boy, his family knew him as Manzi. This nickname had to do with his fondness for chamomile tea. (*Manzanilla* is Spanish for chamomile tea.) In the English-speaking world, however, he would later be known as Cesar Chavez.

Librado bought a group of small buildings—a grocery store, a garage, and a pool hall. Next he cleared 80 acres of land for the man who had sold him the buildings. For his efforts, Librado was told that he would be able to keep 40 of those cleared acres.

Things changed, however, when Librado asked for a deed to the land. It was then that he found out the land had recently been sold. He contacted a lawyer who advised him to buy the property from the new owner. Librado Chavez did, but later he ran into trouble paying the interest on the loan. Then the lawyer bought the land from Librado Chavez and turned around and sold it back to the original owner.

Unfortunately for the Chavez family, their money problems did not end there. Librado Chavez allowed his many relatives and friends in the area to buy groceries on credit at his store. Because of the Great Depression, few had the money to pay him back. In an attempt to pay his creditors, Librado Chavez was forced to sell his buildings.

The Great Depression (1929-39) was causing misery for millions of people. Factories and businesses across the country were going out of business. Those that were still open fired many of their workers or lowered their wages. More than 5,000 banks failed, and people lost their life savings. By 1933, one out of every four workers in the United States was unemployed.

Librado and Juana Chavez took their children (Rita, Cesario, Richard, and Helena) back to Papa Chayo's farm. It was crowded. All six of them had to live in one room of the adobe home. Mama Tella and one of her daughters lived in another part of the house. By this time, Papa Chayo had died. Nevertheless, Cesario and Richard were delighted to get the chance to sleep on a pool table instead of in a bed. The pool table was one thing their father had been unable to sell.

Financial hardship, however, was not the only setback that the Chavez family experienced. Helena, the youngest child, fell ill with severe diarrhea. Apparently it was due to impure drinking water. (The family had been in the habit of placing water from a canal into large metal containers. When the dirt settled to the bottom, the Chavezes used the water.) Helena's diarrhea worsened, leaving her weaker and weaker. A few days later, she was dead. This need for such a basic requirement as clean water is one of the things that drove Cesar Chavez to work so hard in later

During the Great Depression of the 1930s, many farmers lost their farms because they could not pay their bills.

years to improve the standard of living of migrant families.

In spite of many hardships, conditions did get better for the Chavez family. They were able to raise all the food they needed. That was one of the best things about moving back to Papa Chayo's farm. They had corn and squash, melons and beans, tomatoes and chili peppers, and lettuce and grapes. There were a couple of cows, some chickens, and several sheep. There was even enough food left over to barter, or trade for services. When Cesar's sister Vicky was born, for instance, the doctor was paid with a load of watermelons.

Through good times and bad, the Chavez family remained a close one. Librado Chavez showed his sons how to make little cars out of sardine cans and spools. And at night he was the one to fetch glasses of water and hoist a child onto his shoulders for

14

the trip to the outhouse which sheltered the primitive toilet.

"When we worked together as I got older, I would ask questions about all sorts of things," recalled Chavez. "I was always very inquisitive, but he [Chavez's father] was patient, and he would answer me."

With her warmth and wise advice, Juana Chavez was comforting as well. To this day, her *dichos*, or proverbs, remain with her children.

"She would always talk about not fighting. Despite a culture where you're not a man if you don't fight back," said Chavez, "she would say, 'No, it's best to turn the other cheek. God gave you senses like eyes and mind and tongue, and you can get out of anything.' She would say, 'It takes two to fight.' That was her favorite. 'It takes two to fight, and one can't do it alone.' She had all kinds of proverbs for that. 'It's better to say that he ran from here than to say he died here.' When I was young I didn't realize the wisdom in her words, but it has been proved to me so many times since." It was only years later that Cesar Chavez realized that he had first learned about nonviolence from his mother.

"Although my mother opposed violence, I think the thing that she really cracked down on the most was being selfish. She made us share everything we had."

Juana Chavez made it known throughout the area that hoboes were always welcome. *Trampitas*, as the Chavez children called them, had a habit of dropping in around mealtime. These tramps could always count on rice and beans and tortillas, the thin round cakes of cornmeal. They would be served as much as the family had to offer.

In 1934, at the age of seven, Cesario started school. When he entered the three-room schoolhouse, he was immediately called Cesar by the English-speaking teacher. Although most of the 200 children were Spanish-speaking, they were always called by the English equivalent of their names. Cesar did not like school very much. One of the major problems was that the students weren't allowed to speak Spanish. If they did speak Spanish instead of English in the classroom, the teacher often rapped them on their knuckles. For speaking Spanish on the playground, they were sometimes paddled by the principal. What hurt even more,

CESAR CHAVEZ'S CALIFORNIA

N
W ⊕ E
S

SACRAMENTO VALLEY

C E N T R A L

Nevada

● Sacramento

● Stockton
● Berkeley

San Francisco ●

● Modesto

San Jose ●

SANTA CLARA VALLEY

SAN JOAQUIN VALLEY

SALINAS VALLEY

V A L L E Y

● Madera
● Fresno
● Fowler
● Hanford

● Earlimart
● Delano
● MacFarland
● Bakersfield
La Paz ■

TEHACHAPI MOUNTAINS

California

Arizona

Oxnard ●
Los Angeles ●

● Santa Monica

COACHELLA VALLEY

LAGUNA DAM

Brawley ●
IMPERIAL VALLEY

San Diego ●

Yuma

PACIFIC OCEAN

MEXICO

KEY

● CITIES AND TOWNS

50   100   1 inch ≈ 133 miles

though, was what happened when they made a mistake in English. For that they were ridiculed.

"It's a terrible thing," recalled Cesar Chavez, "when you have your own language and customs, and those are shattered. I remember trying to find out who I was and not being able to understand. Once, for instance, I recall saying I was a Mexican. The teacher was quick to correct me. 'Oh, no, don't say that!' she said. But what else could I say? . . . To me an American was a white man."

Unlike Cesar, his older sister, Rita, loved school. "It was only because I didn't have any shoes or any school clothes that I stopped going," she remembered. "Later when my father finally found a job and could get me shoes, I thought I was too old to go back. It's only afterward you realize you're never too old to learn."

Rather than school, Cesar Chavez loved the lessons of the nights during the summertime. Friends and relatives would gather under the stars and talk into the desert darkness.

"Then we heard about the Mexican revolution [1910], the battles fought by farm workers, and how they won and lost. There were stories—a lot of them—about the haciendas, how the big landowners treated the people, about the injustices, the cruelties, the exploitation, the actual experiences our uncles had had."

Anti-Chicano feeling was high during the Great Depression. (*Chicanos* is the term many Americans of Mexican background use to refer to themselves.) Almost 500,000 Mexicans and Mexican Americans were deported. Forcing so many people out of the United States was supposed to help the remaining Americans find jobs more easily. Deporting workers who demanded better working conditions was supposed to help stop labor protests.

Another strong influence on Cesar was religion. His religious training began early. Mama Tella thoroughly prepared Cesar and Rita in their catechism. (This is a set of questions and answers about Christianity learned by Roman Catholics.) They were then quizzed by the nearest priest, 20 miles away in Yuma. After they answered all his questions, they were allowed to receive their First Communion. Communion is the high point of the Roman Catholic mass.

In 1937, $4,000 in taxes that Librado Chavez owed on the

During the Great Depression, thousands of families who had lost their farms traveled to California in search of work.

adobe house and land came due. (That $4,000 could buy about what $27,000 could today.) Unable to raise such a large sum of money in the Yuma area, he drove across the Arizona border into California. He headed north into the Imperial Valley, the Coachella Valley, and along the coast looking for work.

Librado Chavez found beans to harvest in Oxnard and a place to stay. Then he sent word for his family and their relatives to come. With two cousins sharing the driving, the Chavez family joined the stream of migrants flooding into California.

Unlike the Chavez family, many of these migrants were moving to California for a different reason. They were escaping the drought-ridden Great Plains, especially parts of Oklahoma, Texas, Kansas, Colorado, and New Mexico. Poor farming practices and the grazing of too many animals had added to the Great Plains' drought problem. The wind blew the soil into huge dust storms. The land there had turned into what was called the Dust Bowl. These farmers' crops had failed, leaving them practically penniless. They left their Dust Bowl farms and traveled to what they thought would be the land of opportunity—California.

Nevertheless, the result was the same for both the Chavez family and the thousands of Dust Bowl families. Instead of working their own farms, they were now going to be field hands on the huge farms of commercial growers. When one crop was harvested, they would be moving on to the next crop. Their lives would be the opposite of the rooted life of a landowning farmer. They would be leading the rootless life of wanderers.

Cesar Chavez was in for a shock when the family moved into a shack in the *barrio* (the Spanish-speaking neighborhood) of Oxnard. The five Chavez children (Rita, 13; Cesar, 11; Richard, 10; Vicky, 4; and Lenny, 2) had been used to playing on the wide-open land behind the adobe. But now a landlady told them they couldn't play in the fenced-in yard. And when they left a ball outside overnight, it was stolen. "I couldn't understand how it could be stolen—why?" asked Cesar. "To us it was a real tragedy."

Soon after they arrived, Cesar went to the store for a quarter's worth of peppers. The clerk gave him fewer than he should have. When Cesar returned home, Juana Chavez sent him back to the store to complain to the owner. A few days later, the clerk caught Cesar outside the school and beat him up.

"I remember I was afraid of him because he was bigger," recalled Cesar years later, "but besides that there must have been something else that kept me from fighting. Maybe part of it was nonresistance. Probably I was afraid to fight also because of my mother."

As would often be the case for the rest of their schooling, the Chavez children worked half a day and went to school half a day. But their work was far different from the chores they had shared around the ranch. Now it seemed like real work. "There is such a difference," explained Cesar Chavez, "between working for yourself and working for others."

After three months, the family returned to North Gila Valley with the hope of hanging onto their ranch. To help pay the back taxes and interest, the ranch was sold at a public auction in February 1939. Librado Chavez made the highest bid at $2,300 and had 30 days to raise the money. Librado tried but was unable to get a bank loan. Papa Chayo's ranch was bought instead by a nearby grower who had bid $1,750.

It was a sad day when the new owner's tractor arrived at the ranch. Helplessly, the Chavez family watched as the irrigation ditches, which Papa Chayo, Librado, and other members of the family had dug, were filled in. The corral that had once held their horses lay in splinters. The trees they had planted on the ranch were pushed over.

"My dad would never let us carve our initials or do anything to those trees," said Cesar Chavez. "'You shouldn't do that because it's bad,' he'd say. He had taught us to respect nature."

The land that the extended Chavez family had loved and worked for 30 years was no longer theirs. Soon Librado and Juana Chavez and their five children loaded the old Studebaker with all their possessions. Leaving behind the graves of Helena, Papa Chayo, and Mama Tella, the Chavez family headed toward California.

They had become like one of the many families described in John Steinbeck's *The Grapes of Wrath*:

> Those families which had lived on a little piece of land, who had lived and died on forty acres, had eaten or starved on the produce of forty acres, had now the whole West to rove in. And they scampered about, looking for work; and the highways were streams of people, and the ditch banks were lines of people. Behind them more were coming. The great highways streamed with moving people.

To look at things at long range, though, there was one bright spot to the family's misfortune. "If we had stayed there [in Arizona]," realized Cesar Chavez later, "possibly I would have been a grower."

If the Chavez family had not been forced off their land, things would have been different. Or, if the Chavez family had been able to make a decent wage as farm workers, then they would have been able to buy their own land. In either case, the story of Cesar Chavez would be far different. The cause of the migrant farm workers would never have gained its most effective champion.

CHAPTER TWO

Like Migrating Birds

The Chavez family arrived in California with only $40 in their pockets. To find out where work was available, they were at the mercy of the labor contractors. These were the people who recruited workers for the growers. On the advice of one labor

Farm workers load harvested crops onto a truck. During the 1930s, people did this difficult work for less than a dollar a day.

contractor, they drove 50 miles looking for work. When they arrived, they were told that no more workers were needed. Listening to another labor contractor, they drove 100 miles in a different direction. Upon reaching their destination, they found out that the job was already finished.

Librado Chavez found it difficult to understand why these Anglo (white, English-speaking) labor contractors would lie about such things. Why would someone tell falsehoods to total strangers?

Overlooking the ethics involved, the reason was rather simple. Labor contractors received money for the number of workers they supplied to a ranch. Most of these contractors were unconcerned about the status of the job or living conditions. Even to those who were fortunate enough to be working, contractors were known to be dishonest. They often incorrectly weighed the amounts picked, saying the crops weighed less than they did, or subtracted money from the workers' meager wages for benefits that did not exist.

This was a system that weighed heavily in favor of the growers. The migrants had to have jobs because they had to eat. Having so many migrant workers in need of jobs would push low wages down even lower.

This was the situation the Chavez family found themselves trapped in. They were eager to find any stoop labor in the fields they could. During the first year they picked peas for less than a penny a pound. They picked cherries for less than 2 cents a pound. Another time the Chavezes picked peas for 25 cents a day for each of them but had to pay 25 cents each for the ride to the fields. Elsewhere they packed apricots all day and made only 30 cents. By the end of the first year the Chavezes had made no more than $300.

Back in Arizona, the Chavez family had been used to hard work. But there they had been working for themselves. They could sell or eat what they picked. They could choose to work in the early mornings and the late afternoons when it was cooler. They could take breaks when they needed or wanted to. The adults could break up the monotony by doing different jobs. The children could drop what they were doing and return to playing.

All of them could have a drink of water without paying for it.

"I bitterly missed the ranch," recalled Chavez. "Maybe that is when the rebellion started. Some had been born into the migrant stream. But we had been on the land, and I knew a different way of life. We were poor, but we had liberty. The migrant is poor, and he has no freedom."

One of the most unfortunate incidents the Chavezes experienced came during their second year of migrant labor. They were working in a vineyard all by themselves. After the seven-day workweek was over, the labor contractor said that he hadn't yet received the money from the grower. Week after week, the contractor kept saying the same thing. After the seventh week, Librado Chavez went to collect their pay. He knocked on the door only to discover that the contractor had disappeared. The Chavez family had worked almost two months for nothing.

Experiences like these encouraged Librado Chavez to join unions as a show of support to workers everywhere. At one time or another he paid dues to several different unions. If there had been an agricultural union, Librado Chavez would have joined that one, too. "I must have gotten interested in unions through him," said Cesar Chavez.

The living conditions for the Chavez family were no better than their working situations. One time they lived in one room in a barrio of San Jose known as Sal Si Puedes. (This is Spanish for "Get Out If You Can.") Another time they were living in a tent with winter fast approaching. Fortunately, they were rescued by a woman who insisted that they move into one of her cabins.

Although the Chavez family members were around food all day, it was a struggle for them to get enough to eat. (This is one of the heartbreaking ironies in the lives of farm workers.) For one entire winter, they existed on muddy-tasting carp that Librado Chavez speared in a ditch. They ate mustard greens that the boys collected. Occasionally, they were helped by the generosity of other migrant workers who had extra food.

Clothes were almost as scarce as food. Cesar and Richard had only one sweatshirt apiece. On washday they stood in the cold tent until their sweatshirts dried. Their socks never seemed to match either. When they attended school, other students made

24

THE GOVERNOR SENDS
AID TO PIXLEY
24 DEPUTY SHERIFFS
11 HIGHWAY PATROLMEN
WE WANT
FOOD!

Hungry migrant workers during the 1930s. Although they harvested crops, they earned barely enough to buy food.

fun of them about this. Then one day Cesar hit upon the idea of saying it was the latest style. Soon, some of their classmates were wearing mismatched socks, too.

To make some money, Cesar and Richard shined shoes and sold newspapers. But the best job they had was at the local movie theater. Every afternoon after school they swept the floor. At the end of the week, they each received a nickel, plus a pass to the Sunday movie. That was when they got to sit down and enjoy the latest episode of *The Lone Ranger*.

One of the things that produced the most profound effects on young Cesar Chavez was the NO DOGS OR MEXICANS ALLOWED signs posted in diners and restaurants. In Brawley in the southeastern corner of California, there was a diner that was reported to have good hamburgers. Cesar and Richard decided to go in and have something to eat. On the door was a sign that stated WHITE TRADE ONLY. "But we had just come from the country, from Arizona, from a community that was mostly Mexican or whites too poor to bother about us," remembered Cesar. "So we didn't understand yet, and we got up our nerve and went in."

The young woman at the counter just stared at the Chavez brothers as they asked for two hamburgers. "What's the matter, you can't read?" she snapped. As the two young boys fled from the diner, she and her boyfriend laughed at them.

Years later, Cesar recalled, "Richard was cursing them, but I was the one who had spoken to them, and I was crying. That laugh rang in my ears for twenty years—it seemed to cut us out of the human race."

As the Chavez family settled into their new life, what crops they picked changed with the seasons. Like other migrant farm workers, they were "following the crop." Winters they worked with broccoli, cabbage, carrots, cauliflower, lettuce, mustard greens, onions, and peas. Cutting broccoli was cold work because their hands and feet were in water. Weeding lettuce was backbreaking because they had to use a short-handled hoe known as *el cortito*. And the rows of lettuce stretched for miles.

The growers cut the hoe handles short because migrant labor was cheaper than wood. (Also, the growers may have felt the workers would do a better job if they were right on top of their weeding. Whether or not this stoop labor was injurious to the workers was inconsequential.) It was said that the grower believed that the Mexican was the only one who would stoop so low to make a dollar. The reply of the farm worker was that the grower was the only one who would stoop so low to save one.

In late spring, the Chavez family worked with cantaloupes and watermelons. Then it was on to either beans or cherries or apricots. In summer, there were chili peppers, corn, and lima beans to pick. In late summer and fall, there were cucumbers, prunes, tomatoes, and grapes. In the fall and early winter, there was cotton. Then it was back to broccoli again.

Of course, where the Chavez family lived also changed with

the season. They were like migrating birds. During the wintertime they worked in the Imperial Valley near the California-Mexico border. From there they journeyed north toward Stockton and the Sacramento Valley. In between were different growing areas: the Coachella Valley, the Salinas Valley, the San Joaquin Valley, and the Santa Clara Valley. By the winter of the following year, the Chavezes would once again be back in the Imperial Valley.

At some point during their annual migration, the Chavez family must have come to the realization that their dream of saving enough money to buy their own land was rapidly fading. Instead, they were completely involved in the day-to-day struggle for existence.

"As for me, I was at that age where I didn't know what it meant

Migrant workers in California during the 1930s. This difficult work, called stoop labor, involved crops such as lettuce.

to be without land to farm," said Cesar Chavez. "I just felt restricted by all the No Trespassing signs. I felt caged. But I have a hunch my dad suffered more than anybody else, though he never showed it to us." In Spanish, the name *Librado* means "the freed one." Librado Chavez's life was far from free.

The Chavez family, however, did own one thing that was very valuable. That was their ability to work. On occasion they withheld their work to support a protest against an injustice done to others in the field. "We felt good," recalls Cesar. "Lose a day's pay, or two, but we felt we had kept something that belonged to us . . . our dignity."

One day, in a diner, Cesar Chavez stood up to another kind of injustice. He was about 14 at the time. A waitress had been ordered by the manager not to serve the Chavez family because they were not Anglos. As they were beginning to leave, the oldest son stopped.

"No, I have to speak up someday," said Cesar Chavez, "and it's going to be today." Turning to the manager, he said, "Why do you have to treat people like that? A man who behaves like you do is not even a human being!" Although the Chavez family was thrown out of the restaurant, Cesar had stood up to an injustice. It would be the first of many times.

As happens with many teenagers, when Cesar Chavez was himself in his teens, he began to rebel. When he had been younger, he had loved to listen to the stories of older people. Now he sought out the company of people his own age. He even wore the long coat and pegged pants sported by the *pachuco*. The pachucos were the young Mexican Americans who wore flashy clothes and were members of gangs.

"My rebellion as a teen-ager," says Chavez, "was against Mexican music, my mother's herbs [used in folk medicine], and some of her religious ideas. But I didn't say I wasn't a Mexican."

Even in his rebellion, though, his mother influenced his future attitudes. He was to say later: "On the road, no matter how badly off we were, she would never let us pass a guy or a family in trouble. Never. During the Second World War, we began to travel in groups. We'd pick up families that were new, that had just been dumped into the migrant stream. After we sort of gave them an

After attending more than three dozen schools, Cesar Chavez graduated in 1942 from the eighth grade. He was fifteen.

apprenticeship, they felt confident, and they'd take off."

In 1942 at the age of 15, Cesar Chavez graduated from eighth grade. By that time he had attended 37 different schools. Formal education was seeming more and more pointless to him. Besides that, his father had hurt his back, and Cesar didn't want his mother to work in the fields anymore. As the oldest son, Cesar felt it was his duty to help out full-time.

One day as Chavez was bent over in the fields, a small plane swooped low. Suddenly a choking spray of DDT—a powerful insect-killing chemical that was used to protect crops—settled over the plants and the workers below. A man near Chavez collapsed and had to be carried off. In the future, Chavez would see poisoning from chemicals as one of the biggest hazards of all to farm workers.

After work, Chavez often went to an ice-cream shop in Delano specializing in malted milk. "That's where I saw Helen for the first time. I remember she had flowers in her hair. After school, she worked at the People's grocery store, and, of course, I became a very good customer."

That was when he was in town, but he was not in Delano very often. "The crops changed and we kept moving," recalled Chavez. "There was a time for planting, and a time for thinning, and an endless variety of harvests up and down the state, along the coast and in the interior valleys."

In the early 1940s, the United States was involved in World War II then raging in Europe and Asia. In 1944, Chavez's life changed dramatically when he joined the U.S. Navy. At that time young men who did not volunteer for one of the branches of the armed services were being drafted into the army. If Chavez had not joined the navy, he probably would have been drafted into the army. The 17-year-old did it partly to get away from the fields and partly to avoid going into the army.

After basic training in San Diego, Chavez was sent to Saipan, a naval base on an island in the South Pacific. However, the life of a deckhand on a destroyer escort on weather patrol did not appeal to him. It did not seem to Chavez to be much of an improvement over the life of a farm worker.

One of the most significant things to happen to him during

Spraying crops with chemicals to kill crop-destroying insects. By the 1940s, many workers had been exposed to pesticides.

this time occurred when he was on leave back in Delano. Chavez went to a local theater to see a movie. Instead of sitting on the side where the Mexican and Filipino Americans were supposed to sit, Chavez sat on the Anglo side of the theater. The manager spotted the teen and told him to move. When Chavez refused, the manager called in the police. Two policemen removed Chavez from his seat and took him to jail.

The desk sergeant did not know what charge to write down. Should it be trespassing? The young man had bought a ticket. Should it be disturbing the peace? He had been quietly watching the movie. The sergeant telephoned a lawyer. After a brief conversation, he phoned a judge. Eventually, the sergeant lectured Chavez for an hour and let him go.

It was one more experience that Chavez would be able to draw upon later. It illustrated what happened when a strong moral right came into conflict with a weaker legal right.

When his two years in the military were over, Chavez went back to the San Joaquin Valley. Chavez returned to working in cotton fields, fruit orchards, and vineyards. The conditions had not improved. If anything, they seemed even worse. Chavez was now more aware of how unfair the system was.

One of the brightest moments in Cesar Chavez's life took place in 1948. Four years after they had first met, a time during which they were often apart for long periods because of harvests and his hitch in the navy, Cesar Chavez and Helen Fabela had grown closer. An infatuation had grown into love and now a commitment. On October 22, 1948, 21-year-old Cesar married 20-year-old Helen.

For their honeymoon, the couple borrowed the family's old Studebaker and traveled to many of California's Spanish missions. From San Diego to Sonoma, they visited the thick-walled adobe churches for two weeks. They marveled at the tiled roofs and clay floors of these 200-year-old structures. The missions' construction was similar to the adobe house built by his father and Papa Chayo back in Arizona.

The couple moved to a farm outside of San Jose and tried the life of sharecroppers. A sharecropper is a tenant farmer who receives an agreed-upon part of the crop he or she grows on the owner's land. However, there are often deductions for seeds, tools, living quarters, and food.

In 1949, Helen and Cesar's first child, Fernando, was born. So they tried even harder to make money raising strawberries. But whether as migrant farm workers or as sharecroppers, it was a difficult life.

In 1947, the National Farm Labor Union (NFLU) had called a strike against the DiGiorgio Fruit Corporation. The strikers wanted a 10-cent raise. They also demanded a seniority system in which workers with the most years of service would receive special consideration for promotions and pay increases. In addition, they also wanted a system for expressing worker complaints and recognition of their union as the official group representing the farm workers. In violation of the law, DiGiorgio brought in Mexican nationals to replace the striking workers. The company was able to break the strike.

In 1949, the San Joaquin Valley Agriculture Labor Bureau, a state agency with representatives from six counties that oversaw local farm problems, lowered the payment for picking 100 pounds of cotton from $3.00 to $2.50. The National Farm Labor Union again called a strike.

Cesar Chavez went to the NFLU meetings, which were held every day for two weeks. "Some very good stuff was developed at these meetings, but I wanted to do more than just be there. I wanted to help. I didn't know anything about unions." Although Chavez found the strike lacking in organization, the NFLU still achieved its goal of returning the payment for picking 100 pounds of cotton back up to $3.00.

In November 1949, a special subcommittee of the U.S. House of Representatives' Education and Labor Committee held a hearing on the DiGiorgio strike. Chavez traveled to Bakersfield to attend the two-day hearing to learn all he could.

Richard M. Nixon was a Republican congressman from California on this subcommittee. (Nixon would later become the President of the United States, serving from 1969 until he resigned in 1974.) After two days of testimony, Nixon summed up the position of the subcommittee, as well as of the growers. He spoke out against the union in these words:

Agriculture labor has been exempted from all labor relations ever written. The evidence before the subcommittee shows that it would be harmful to the public interest and to all responsible labor unions to legislate otherwise. . . . [T]he subcommittee finds that the exemption of agriculture labor from the labor management relations act is sound.

In the summer of 1950, Chavez and his brother Richard went to northern California to work in a lumber camp close to the Oregon border. Eventually, it might have led to a better life for their families. They might have built houses and a new life there. "We thought the only way we could get out of the circle of poverty was to work our way up and send our kids to college," said Cesar Chavez. The circle of poverty is "the trap most poor people get themselves into."

But for Cesar Chavez, the life of sun and soil was extremely important. So, he and his brother decided to return. Besides, his interests lay with the struggle of the farm workers. "It's easier for a person to just escape, to get out of poverty," he once said, "than to change the situation." Chavez wanted to change things.

CHAPTER THREE

Becoming an Organizer

Cesar Chavez was beginning to realize that there were only two solutions to the dilemma of the migrant workers. "Either the employers begin to see the workers as human beings, or the workers organize against the employers and demand changes."

Helen and Cesar Chavez rented a small house in Sal Si Puedes in San Jose. Cesar Chavez found work in a lumberyard and in the orchards around San Jose. In 1950, their daughter Sylvia was born. The next year, Linda was born. With their growing family, the Chavezes were even more concerned about the future.

Father Donald McDonnell came to their barrio to be priest to the many Mexican Americans living there. Chavez immediately liked this Roman Catholic priest, who was about his own age. He spent all the time he could with McDonnell. "We had long talks about farm workers," said Chavez. "I knew a lot about the work, but I didn't know anything about the economics, and I learned quite a bit from him."

"And then we did a lot of reading," recalled Chavez. "That's when I started reading the Encyclicals [letters from the pope to the bishops of the Roman Catholic Church], St. Francis [the founder of the Franciscan order], and Gandhi [the leader who helped free India from Britain by using nonviolent methods] and having the case for attaining social justice explained."

Chavez learned how the Chinese became the first migrant farm laborers in the western states and territories. They had worked in the mines and on the transcontinental railroad. When the gold rush ended and the last spike had been driven in 1869, many of them turned to farm work. In the 1880s, a U.S. treaty with China permitted the United States to regulate and limit the number of Chinese workers entering the country. In 1882, Congress passed a law prohibiting Chinese immigration for 10 years. Despite those measures, in 1886, there were 30,000 Chinese working in the fields. With the serious depression of 1893, resentment rose against the Chinese for having jobs and businesses. The Chinese already had lost most of their jobs in the fields. An 1894 treaty between China and the United States recognized a new 10-year period during which Chinese immigration to the United States was prohibited.

Japanese workers made up the next large group of farm laborers. At their peak between 1890 and 1920, there were 72,000 Japanese farm workers. They were not only hard workers but also good farmers. They were well organized and went on to succeed in their situation. They even bought farms of their own. But in 1913, California passed a state law limiting the right of the Japanese to own farmland. In 1920, California limited their right to rent farmland. By 1924, the U.S. Congress had officially excluded their entry into the United States. (Most Japanese immigration had already been stopped by means of a secret "Gentlemen's Agreement" between the United States and Japan in 1907.)

In the mid-1920s, Filipinos were recruited from the Philippines and Hawaii. By 1930, there were 25,000 single Filipino men working as farm laborers in California. Their hope was to save enough money to send for their families. Before that happened, though, attention was turned to another labor pool.

During the Great Depression of the 1930s, the Dust Bowl sent 130,000 Americans displaced from their homes in the southwestern Great Plains into California. These people—mostly poor whites and African Americans—became the next group of farm workers. Many improved their lot in life and got other jobs. But there were still more than enough farm workers to supply the agricultural business. In fact, during the Great Depression, several hundred thousand Mexicans and Mexican Americans were deported, that is, forced by the U.S. government to return to Mexico. World War II changed all that. Many men were drafted as soldiers. Women and older men worked in factories making weapons and war supplies.

So finally, practically by default, the need for farm laborers had fallen to Mexicans and Mexican Americans to fill. During World War II, the federal government had started the new *bracero*

During the 1920s, thousands of Filipino farm workers came from
the Philippines and Hawaii to work in California.

program to make up for the shortage of farm workers. (The literal meaning of *bracero* is "arm-men.") This program was a way to hire Mexican nationals to pick certain crops for the length of the harvest or to work in industries for a limited time. When the seasonal work was over, the braceros returned home to Mexico. In 1945, at the end of the war, there were 50,000 braceros working under this program.

Nevertheless, after the war was over, the use of braceros continued. One problem with the program was that it pushed wages down. When many workers are available for fewer jobs, they often are willing to work for less. Although most Americans considered the wages to be low, most Mexicans considered them high when compared to what they could earn in Mexico. Americans were reluctant to enter the fields, whereas Mexicans found it difficult to get out. So, if few Americans could be found to work at these wages, then there was a need for even more braceros.

Another problem with the bracero program was that it encouraged illegal immigration. By 1953, there were 200,000 braceros. Another 800,000 Mexican nationals were captured by the U.S. Border Patrol attempting to cross over into the United States. Many of those who slipped through became field workers. Obviously, these were people who would never be able to complain about low wages, poor treatment, or horrible living conditions. For if they protested, they could be turned over to the authorities and sent back to Mexico.

In June 1952, Fred Ross was in Sal Si Puedes to start a local chapter of the Community Service Organization (CSO). The CSO had been started in the barrios of East Los Angeles in 1946. It was a private agency to help minority groups, including migrant workers, learn how to improve their lives.

Fred Ross had heard about Cesar Chavez from a nurse who had been with Helen during the delivery of one of their children. When Ross had gone around to the Chavez house and knocked, Chavez pretended not to be at home. For the next few days he avoided Ross. Chavez thought the tall, thin Anglo was just another person doing research on the barrio, a do-gooder who would disappear after collecting all the information he needed.

Chavez explained on another occasion how the farm worker feels: "Gee, I may be poor, but I got a lot of dignity, and I don't need to be felt sorry for." In other words, "look at the farm workers as human beings."

In spite of the lack of response, Ross kept trying. Finally, Chavez talked to him. Ross did not look like a do-gooder. With his work clothes, boots, and stubble of beard, he seemed more like a farm worker. Chavez agreed to hold a meeting in his home in order to teach Ross a lesson. He invited some local toughs to the house meeting to give this tall Anglo a hard time.

On the night of the house meeting, things turned out differently. Fred Ross started off by speaking in Spanish. He even sounded like a Mexican.

At one point Fred Ross began talking about the *Bloody Christmas* case. "He knew the problems as well as we did," admitted Chavez. Everyone in the room was probably familiar with this case of police officers beating up Mexican Americans at a jail in Los Angeles. However, they had not known a key element. The Community Service Organization had been responsible for getting six of the police officers suspended.

At another point Ross asked what the biggest industry in California was. When no one guessed correctly, he told them. It was agriculture. In 1951, California growers made over $2 billion. In the same year, the average migrant family barely made $2,000. That was at a time when the average annual wages for one non-farm worker came to about $3,200.

There was definitely a need for change. And where, wondered Ross, would the leadership for this change come from? It would certainly not be from the Anglo community. The leadership for change would have to come from the Chicanos themselves. Chavez was so taken with what Ross was saying that he went along with him that very night to another house meeting.

Later, Fred Ross wrote in his journal:

> To the home of Cesar Chavez: very responsive. Agreed to become a deputy registrar. Chavez has real push. Understanding. Loyalty and Enthusiasm. Grassroots leadership quality.

Ross's journal entry would serve as a good thumbnail assessment of Cesar Chavez's future effectiveness.

In the next few weeks, Chavez came home from the orchards and went out to meetings with Ross at night. Chavez soaked up everything he could about how Ross worked.

"As time went on, Fred became sort of my hero. I saw him organize, and I wanted to learn. Right away I began to see that organizing was difficult."

Chavez studied how Ross ran house meetings. He watched how Ross got and kept people's attention. He learned how Ross was able to move people from simply being interested to being committed and involved.

"I wanted to do it just as he did," said Chavez, "so I began to learn. It was a beautiful part of my life."

When it came time to register Mexican Americans to vote, Chavez plunged into the task wholeheartedly. Ross even had to ask him to take time off or Chavez would have worked all 85 days of the registration drive. By the end of the drive, Chavez and his fellow deputy registrars had signed up 6,000 new voters.

These people were qualified to vote. However, the Republicans working at the voting places asked them questions such as whether or not they could read. This frightened them away from the election polls. (The Republican Central Committee was concerned about these new voters. They feared they could become a group powerful enough to change the outcome of elections.)

Ross wanted to send a telegram to protest this harassment to a U.S. attorney general. The members of the CSO board declined to sign. They felt it would hurt their careers. The only one who would sign was Cesar Chavez. The telegram may not have changed the behavior of the Republican Central Committee, but it showed Cesar Chavez's courage.

When 42-year-old Fred Ross had first met 25-year-old Cesar Chavez, he had written in his journal: "I think I've found the guy I'm looking for." Now he was sure of it.

Ross convinced Saul Alinsky, the director of the Industrial Areas Foundation, to hire Chavez. (The Industrial Areas Foundation was the parent organization of the CSO.) From now

Over the years, Fred Ross (left) worked closely with Cesar Chavez.
He had recruited Chavez as a labor organizer in 1952.

on, Cesar Chavez would not be working in the fields. He would be making $35 a week working as an organizer for the Community Service Organization.

On one of the first days as an organizer, Chavez drove to an address on a side street in West Oakland. He was on time, but he was nervous. Instead of going inside for the house meeting, he simply sat in the car. Finally, he got up his nerve and got out of the car.

Joining the 10 or so people sitting in the living room, he did not say anything. After several minutes, someone wondered out loud when the organizer would arrive. At long last Chavez admitted that he was the person they were waiting for. Cesar Chavez smiled faintly. Like the other people in the room, he was dressed casually. Unlike the others, he was incredibly nervous. It was

41

almost as if his life were on the line. Perhaps what he was experiencing was something similar to stage fright.

"That meeting was a disaster, really a disaster," acknowledged Chavez. "I fumbled all over the place, I was so frightened."

By the end of the meeting, though, the soft-spoken Chavez had convinced his listeners. At least one person was eager to get involved. And another house meeting was already being planned. As the days went on, Chavez began to recruit more people to help register voters. Also, he was finding it a bit easier to lead house meetings.

The person who had helped Chavez the most was Fred Ross. Chavez had watched Ross in action as the older organizer led meetings. Chavez had learned about parliamentary law, the rules used to conduct meetings. He had listened to the effectiveness of using short sentences in Spanish sprinkled with key words in English. (These were words they needed to know since the growers all spoke English.) He had found out the importance of knowing the other side of an argument. He had learned to back up his statements with facts.

Chavez was also reading more. He read John Steinbeck's novel *The Grapes of Wrath* and Walt Whitman's book of poetry *Leaves of Grass*. He also read Jack London's article "Definition of a Strikebreaker" and his novel *The People of the Abyss*. Chavez was beginning to get on his own the education he had never been able to get in school. He was particularly struck by one passage from London's *People of the Abyss*. Cesar Chavez saw the following words as a rule to live by:

> I took with me simple criteria with which to measure. That which made for more life, for physical and spiritual health, was good; that which made for less life, which hurt, dwarfed and distorted life, was bad.

And finally there was Mohandas Karamchand Gandhi. The writings of Mahatma Gandhi were to have a profound effect on Cesar Chavez. (*Mahatma* means a person who is revered for wisdom and selflessness.) Gandhi was considered the father of his country, India. He had been the leader of the Indian people's struggle for independence from Great Britain. Gandhi had used civil disobedience as one of his methods. He had refused to obey British demands and laws, but in a nonviolent way, in order to force the British to give in.

"In my opinion nonviolence is not passivity in any shape or

Gandhi's methods of nonviolent protests against the British rulers in India inspired Chavez.

form," wrote Gandhi. "Nonviolence, as I understand it, is the most active force in the world."

It was through reading the works of Gandhi that Chavez strengthened his own beliefs in nonviolence. Chavez also seemed to like Gandhi's simple life-style. Both men had few possessions to weigh them down.

After Chavez conducted house meetings, there were usually a few people who wanted to stay around afterward to talk. They were coming to Chavez for help. Helping people was something that just came naturally to Cesar Chavez. It was something his parents, especially his mother, had always done.

"Well, one night it just hit me," said Chavez. "Once you helped people most became very loyal. . . . Once I realized helping people was an organizing technique, I increased that work."

After three months of house meetings, Chavez felt it was time to hold a general meeting. Everything was set. As the hour drew close, Chavez wondered if anyone would show up. Seven o'clock came, and a few people drifted in. Then more came. When people stopped arriving, no fewer than 368 people had gathered. "I had become an organizer, I guess," realized Chavez.

On His Own

Because of his work as an organizer, Cesar Chavez and his family would live in a place for three or four months, then move on. Madera, Bakersfield, Hanford—the list of towns lengthened.

"Everywhere there were problems," said Chavez. "There were fights, there were countless cases where we could help people. But no matter what happened, I learned."

Chavez worked 14 hours a day, 7 days a week. "The only way I know," said Chavez, "is to spend an awful lot of time with each individual—hours and hours—until he understands and you've got him going." Even with his salary increase from $35 to $58 a week, it was a struggle to support a family that would soon number eight children.

It was also difficult for Cesar Chavez to be as good a parent as he might have liked. All the traveling, all the late hours made it difficult for him to spend much time with his children. One time his son Paul finally did something to get his father's attention. "One night when I went to bed," remembered Cesar Chavez, "I lay there looking up at the ceiling. I don't know how he reached up there, but right above my bed, where I could not miss it, he wrote 'Paul.'"

Nevertheless, Chavez had to limit the amount of time he spent with his immediate family so that he could give more time to all the others around him. He did not spend time with just a few at the top. He had time for everyone.

"Fred taught me in organizing never to go to the so-called leadership, but to go right down to the grass roots and develop leaders there." As soon as the voter registration drive was completed, the citizenship classes were started. Then it was off to the next place.

One problem that came up time and again was being accused of being a Communist. The McCarthy era was during the early

Cesar Chavez (second from the right) with other Community Service Organization workers.

1950s. Joseph McCarthy, a U.S. senator from Wisconsin, accused many people of being Communists. But he rarely backed up his claims with solid evidence. Anyone who was working to register voters left themselves open to this charge. Why? Because it might alter the status quo—the way things were.

For instance, take the first registration drive Chavez worked on. This had threatened the Republican candidates, who were supported by the growers in the area around Sal Si Puedes. The Republican Central Committee spread a false rumor to the newspapers that Chavez and the CSO were Communists. For a while, wherever he went, Chavez had to explain that he was working for the farm worker, not for the Kremlin. (The Kremlin is a building in Moscow that looks like a fort and served as the center of government for the former Soviet Union.)

In 1958, Cesar Chavez tackled another kind of problem. In organizing a voter registration drive in Oxnard, California, he found out that no local workers could get jobs. Instead, 28,000 braceros had all the work. Chavez set out to find the reason why.

Chavez went to the Farm Placement Service office when it opened at eight o'clock and filled out all the paperwork to apply for work. (This agency was responsible for deciding who was eligible for farm work.) Then he traveled several miles to the nearest bracero camp. He was told that the hiring had begun at four in the morning and had been completed by six. The next morning Chavez returned to the bracero camp. This time he was not hired because his paperwork was out-of-date. It was dated from the day before. On the other hand, the paperwork for the braceros did not expire each day.

It was clear that the government regulations were preventing the local workers from getting hired, so that the growers could hire braceros only. The growers could legally use braceros if local workers were unavailable. The nearby growers wanted braceros because they would work for only 75 cents per hour. At that time, the federal government had no minimum wage requirements for farm workers. Nonfarm workers, on the other hand, could be paid no less than $1.00 an hour. The policy of hiring braceros was repeated elsewhere, too. In 1959, there were 437,000 braceros in the United States.

Every morning Chavez showed up at the Farm Placement Service to fill out all the forms. Soon there were others, sometimes as many as 20, joining him. Every morning they filled out all the paperwork. Sometimes it took all day long.

Finally, Chavez called for an investigation. When state officials asked for evidence, Chavez showed the forms. All together, there were almost 2,000 filled-out forms. However, nothing was done. There were still no jobs for local workers.

Chavez then led a sit-in at a local ranch. Some of the CSO members were hired, but they were fired a few hours later.

In frustration, Chavez organized a candlelight parade. Beginning with only a few hundred people, there were over 10,000 marchers by the end. "That's when I discovered the power of the march," said Chavez.

Investigation followed investigation. Eventually, several people at the Farm Placement Service, including the director, were fired. Growers even started coming to the CSO office at Oxnard to get workers. Chavez's office had turned into an employment hall. The time was ripe to form a union. But when Chavez suggested it, the CSO rejected the idea.

"We could have built a union there, but the CSO wouldn't approve," remembered Cesar Chavez. "In fact, the whole project soon fell apart. I wanted to go for a strike and get some contracts, but the CSO wouldn't let me." As more and more of the leadership of the CSO came from the middle class, they had become reluctant to try new ideas. The CSO also considered itself to be a civic organization rather than a union.

Chavez thought of quitting and forming a union of his own. "But then," realized Chavez, "maybe I wasn't ready. If I had been, I would have done it even though CSO was against it." Instead, in 1960 Chavez was appointed as national director of the CSO, a position he accepted. His new job was at the headquarters in Los Angeles. His salary was increased to $150 a week, plus expenses. Nevertheless, Chavez could not forget about the idea of forming a union for farm workers.

Two years later at the CSO national convention, Chavez again tried to get the CSO to back a union. It was voted down. Two weeks later, on his 35th birthday, March 31, 1962, Cesar Chavez

48

resigned as national director of the Community Service Organization. His announcement caught many staff members by surprise. However, there had been several clues scattered along the way. Chavez had been attending meetings wearing crumpled plaid shirts and work pants. His face had been unshaven, his hair uncut. He was trying to remind others that the CSO was representing hardworking field hands.

"I worked with the CSO for ten years—they taught me how to organize. Then they got pretty middle class, didn't want to go into the fields. So I left."

After months of thinking it over, Chavez had decided to strike out in a new direction. A labor union, the Agricultural Workers Organizing Committee (AWOC), had offered him $200 a week to be an organizer for them. The Peace Corps had offered him twice as much to work for them in South America. (The Peace Corps is an agency of the U.S. government that trains volunteers to work and to help people in less developed countries.)

Helen and Cesar Chavez went on a camping trip with their eight children—Fernando, Sylvia, Linda, Eloise, Anna, Paul, Elizabeth, and Anthony. The trip gave Helen, Cesar, and their children an opportunity to discuss their choices and make up their minds. They talked about the offers from the Agricultural Workers Organizing Committee and the Peace Corps. They talked about what Cesar wanted to accomplish in his life. After two days of discussions, they decided he would not work for the AWOC or the Peace Corps. Chavez should follow his dream. He should work full-time for the farm workers.

So with only $1,200 in savings, the Chavezes moved back to the only place they could really call home. In April 1962, they returned to the city of 14,000 in the heart of the San Joaquin Valley: Delano.

Delano was a place they knew well. The business district was on two streets that ran parallel to Highway 99 and the Southern Pacific Railroad tracks. The town was divided in half. The middle-class Anglos lived on one side of town. The Mexicans, Filipinos, African Americans, and Puerto Ricans, lived on the other.

Delano was a place where many people who worked in the surrounding 38,000 acres of vineyards lived. These workers had

Cesar and Helen Chavez with six of their eight children. The Chavez family moved back to Delano, California, in 1962.

skills that were in demand year-round. The average family income was $2,400, higher than in most places. Many of these workers owned their own homes and sent their children to local schools. They were more stationary than the average farm workers. So, it might be easier to form a union in Delano.

There were also family members in Delano who could help out. Richard Chavez, Cesar's brother, lived nearby. Helen had family members in the area. This was important for the large Chavez family.

Cesar Chavez rented a small house on Kensington Street for his family. Then he headed back toward the fields of the Central Valley. For three days he drove the dusty roads in their old beat-up station wagon. There were many growers around Delano. The two biggest ranches were the 5,000-acre ranch owned by Schenley Industries and the 4,400-acre ranch owned by the DiGiorgio Fruit Corporation.

Chavez observed the workers bent over under the hot sun. They were using *el cortito*, the short-handled hoe. The rows of crops stretched out over the flat farmland as far as the eye could see.

Cesar Chavez was returning to grass-roots organizing. It was something he enjoyed and did well. Chavez was laying the necessary groundwork for what would later become the National Farm Workers Association (NFWA). It was no mistake that the word *union* was not a part of the name. Unions for farm workers had failed in the past. Most recently the AWOC had made an unsuccessful attempt. Chavez wanted a fresh start. He wanted to pull together his family of farm workers from the ground up.

"At first I was frightened . . . ," admits Chavez, after resigning his job in order to start a union for farm workers. "But by the time I had missed the fourth paycheck and found things were still going, that the moon was still there and the sky and the flowers, I began to laugh. I really began to feel free. It was one of my biggest triumphs in terms of finding myself and of being able to discipline myself."

The Chavez family moved into the two-bedroom house on Kensington Street in Delano. The garage was turned into an office. Cesar Chavez traveled the roads in his station wagon. He located farm workers in the fields. He knocked on their doors after work. He asked questions. He organized house meetings. Slowly, he began to build interest in the idea of a union. Back in his garage-office, he would look at a map. His plans were to visit every town and farming camp in the 200-mile-long, 60-mile-wide San Joaquin Valley. That was a total of 86 towns and camps. Soon, however, he knew he would need help. One person can only do so much.

Unfortunately, there was almost no money to pay people. It was a system of sharing and helping. It was built on Chavez's quiet power of persuasion, as well as the power of an idea whose time had come. As Chavez put it: "[I]t's beautiful to give up material things that take up your time, for the sake of time to help your fellow human beings."

One person he contacted to help was his cousin Manuel Chavez, who had lived with his family back in Arizona. Manuel took a six-month leave of absence from selling cars in San Diego.

Grape pickers. From an office in his garage, Chavez began the difficult job of organizing such workers in the Delano area.

Immediately, his salary dropped from $1,500 a month to $5 a week, plus room and board. Manuel Chavez must have surprised even himself. He became so involved with the new union that he never went back to the car lot.

Another person who joined the effort was Gilbert Padillo from the Community Service Organization. And then there was Dolores Huerta. The mother of seven children, Huerta was a tireless worker. She had worked as a lobbyist for the CSO at the state capital in Sacramento. Huerta left her job to work full-time for what would soon be the NFWA.

There was another person who helped—the Reverend Jim Drake, who was assigned by the Migrant Ministry of the National Council of Churches. Chris Hartmire, the executive director of that organization, also helped at every opportunity.

Drake later admitted that he had great doubts about Chavez's chances of success. "I really thought Cesar was crazy," Jim Drake said. "Everybody did except Helen. They had so many children and so little to eat, and that old 1953 Mercury station wagon gobbled up gas and oil. Everything he wanted to do seemed impossible. He used his tiny garage as his headquarters, but it was so hot in there, all the ink melted down in the mimeograph machine I lent him."

Cesar Chavez's commitment was soon tested by the offer of money. This included a $50,000 grant from the Migrant Ministry, the Teamsters, which is a powerful union, and the AFL-CIO, the organization to which many unions belong. Even though there were no restrictions, Chavez refused the offer. He didn't want the brand-new union to feel it had to show immediate results. Also, he wanted the union to be built by the workers themselves.

Although the Reverend Jim Drake had been skeptical in the beginning, he changed his mind the more he saw Chavez in action. "What impressed me was that even though Cesar was desperate," said Drake, "he didn't want our money, or Teamster money, or AFL-CIO money, or any other money that might compromise him. Right from the start, he made it clear that his organization would be independent. And I was impressed by his perseverance. Building the union was a slow, plodding thing based on hard work and very personal relationships."

Field by field, house by house, the small band of organizers crisscrossed the San Joaquin Valley. The people they talked to helped out as well. For no matter how poor the family, there was always some food for these hardworking organizers. Even the children in the Chavez family helped. After school and on weekends, they handed out leaflets. Chavez would drive them to an area where the union needed to find support. The Chavez children would do the rest.

Slowly, the word got around. Interest built to the point that on September 30, 1962, a convention was held in Fresno. A total of 280 farm workers from 65 farming communities attended as voting delegates. Among those in the audience was Cesar Chavez's

The eagle was chosen as the symbol for the farm workers. The Spanish word *huelga* means "strike."

teacher, adviser, and friend: Fred Ross. Ross would eventually leave CSO and join forces with Chavez.

At one of the first meetings a giant flag was unveiled. It featured a black eagle over a white circle on a deep red background. The eagle had been chosen because it is the symbol for both Mexico and the United States. Also, it was the sacred bird of the Aztecs. (In the 14th century the Aztecs had built a strong civilization in the area of what is today Mexico City. That was 200 years before the arrival of the Spanish *conquistadores*, or conquerors.)

Richard Chavez had come up with the idea of using square lines for the eagle, five steps for each wing. This would make it easier to draw. As the flag became the rallying symbol, everyone would be able to make one. Cesar Chavez had suggested the colors. They were bold and eye-catching. Also, flags of red and black in Mexico are used to show there is a strike going on.

By the end of the convention, the delegates had voted to organize a union for farm workers. Cesar Chavez would be the president. Dolores Huerta and Gilbert Padillo would be vice presidents. Manuel Chavez would be the treasurer. The delegates had also adopted the flag, a constitution, and a motto: *Viva La Causa* (Long Live the Cause). "The Cause" was obtaining better wages and working conditions for farm workers. The dues would be $3.50 a month. The National Farm Workers Association had become official.

CHAPTER FIVE

On the National Stage

The long days and nights of organizing were interrupted by the assassination of President John F. Kennedy on November 22, 1963. As it did with so many other people, this murder sickened Chavez. However, it did strengthen his belief in the importance of nonviolence.

By 1964 the National Farm Workers Association (NFWA) had grown stronger. There were 1,000 members and an official newspaper called *El Malcriado*. (The name is Spanish for "a crying child, or one who protests loudly." Or it could be simply translated as "The Mischievous One" or "The Impolite One.") Part of the dues went for a fund to provide burial benefits. A credit union was also set up so that members could borrow small amounts of money.

Chavez's garage office was no longer big enough for the growing union. An old stucco building was located on the west side of town. NFWA members worked at night and on weekends repairing and painting this former grocery store. Richard Chavez built a desk for his brother's office. On the walls of the office were hung pictures of Zapata (a leader of the Mexican Revolution), Gandhi, and Martin Luther King, Jr. This building would now serve as the new NFWA headquarters.

In 1965, there were a million farm workers in the United States. It was a very large group to be without a legal federal minimum wage and the powers of collective bargaining.

On September 8, 1965, a rival to the National Farm Workers Association went on strike. This rival union was the Agricultural Workers Organizing Committee (AWOC). AWOC was made up almost 100 percent of Filipino-American workers. On the other hand, the NFWA was about 90 percent Chicano.

Protesting the low wages of grape pickers, the 800 striking members of AWOC were demanding $1.40 per hour. This would

In 1965, the legal minimum wage for nonfarm workers was $1.50 an hour. Farm workers could legally be paid less.

be an increase of 15 cents. They had been making that previously in the vineyards north of Delano. Larry Itliong, the head of the AWOC, wanted to know if the NFWA would go out on strike, too.

At first Chavez felt the National Farm Workers Association was not yet ready for a strike. They only had 1,200 members and less than $100 in the treasury. More than one agricultural union had failed after going on strike before they were ready. It took a great deal of preparation and organization to handle the strain of a strike.

In addition, the new union would lose a $268,000 antipoverty grant from the U.S. government. The government provided this money for programs designed to help end poverty, but it would not be fair if taxpayers' money was used to support one side in a strike. Nevertheless, the more Chavez thought about it, the more necessary it seemed for the NFWA to support the AWOC and go out on strike.

A general meeting of the NFWA was set for September 16, Mexican Independence Day. (Mexico had won its freedom from Spain on September 16, 1820.) The meeting hall of the white stucco Our Lady of Guadalupe Church was decorated with posters of Emiliano Zapata, the Mexican revolutionary. (Helen Chavez's father had been a colonel during the Mexican Revolution under Pancho Villa.) Emiliano Zapata was remembered by those assembled for statements such as this: "The land belongs to everyone like the air, the water, the light and the heat of the sun; and all who work the land with their own hands have a right to it."

Copies of American writer Jack London's "Definition of a Strikebreaker" were also posted on the walls. "After God had finished the rattlesnake, the toad and the vampire, He had some awful substance left with which He made a strikebreaker," declared these leaflets. "There is nothing lower than a strikebreaker."

Cesar Chavez looked out at the members of the union and then spoke in his quiet voice. "We are engaged in another struggle for the freedom and dignity which poverty denies us. But it must not be a violent struggle, even if violence is used against us. Violence can only hurt us and our cause."

Cries of "Viva la Huelga!" (Long Live the Strike!) and "Viva Chavez!" filled the air. The National Farm Workers Association voted to support the strike.

On September 20, 1965, pickets from the NFWA joined AWOC in front of the DiGiorgio, Giumarra, and Schenley ranches. The two unions had the herculean task of positioning 1,200 workers to strike 34 growers whose land spread out over 400 square miles of vineyards. In addition, the strikers had to be fed. The small children of striking mothers had to be cared for. Medical care had to be provided.

"If a man comes out of the field and goes on the picket line, even for one day, he'll never be the same," said Chavez. "The picket line is the best possible education."

Certainly it was often an education of hard knocks. Some of the growers became frustrated and took out their anger on the strikers. Punches were thrown, shotguns were fired overhead, and even pesticides were sprayed on the strikers. Sometimes it became difficult for the strikers not to fight back. Cesar Chavez would have to counsel them on the importance of having the strike remain nonviolent. And every time the growers reacted violently, there was more publicity to win people to their cause.

Viva La Causa means "Long LIve the Cause."

"Here was Cesar," observed Luis Valdez, who had started the Farm Workers Theater, "burning with a patient fire, poor like us, dark like us, talking quietly. . . . We didn't know it until we met him, but he was the leader we had been waiting for."

On October 19, forty-four people were arrested on the picket lines by the Kern County sheriff's officers. Among those arrested for "unlawful public assembly" was Helen Chavez. This was the first of many arrests

Helen Chavez was one of the first picketers to be arrested in the long grape workers' strike that began in 1965.

of strikers during the five-year grape strike. When newspapers carried news of the arrest, many American citizens became concerned. Wasn't this arrest in violation of the strikers' First Amendment rights? Didn't this violate "the right of the people peaceably to assemble"? Wasn't this "abridging the freedom of speech"? Robert F. Kennedy, the senator from New York, believed it was.

Word of the strike and the arrests spread across college campuses. Chavez traveled to several campuses to win support for the union. At the University of California at Berkeley, Chavez suggested that students donate the money they would have spent on lunch that day. They immediately contributed $6,700. The money was used to help buy food to feed the strikers.

College students began to arrive daily in Delano to help in

whatever way they could. In addition to college students, Chavez appealed to others to help the farm workers in their struggle. Members of important African-American civil rights groups, such as the Student Nonviolent Coordinating Committee (SNCC) and the Congress of Racial Equality (CORE), arrived to help. Religious leaders, especially from the National Council of Church's Migrant Ministry, also came to their aid.

Chavez was already planning for the effects of the strike to reach beyond the fields of the ranches. Pickets from NFWA were seen as far away as the docks in San Francisco. The longshoremen, members of the International Longshoremen's and Warehousemen's Union, honored the picket lines by refusing to cross these picket lines to load grapes onto ships. This caused the growers great concern. Large quantities of grapes spoiling in warehouses could spell financial disaster for the growers.

An even more effective tool than the strike was the grape boycott, the refusal to buy grapes. The boycott combined with the strike could be even more effective than a strike alone. If no one bought table grapes, then it would not matter whether it had been a good growing season or a bad one. It would not matter how many grapes had been picked in the vineyard and shipped to the stores. It would not even matter whether there had been a successful strike or not. The end result would be the same. If the consumers supported the union demands by not buying grapes, the growers would be ruined financially.

Chavez sent a boycott staff of workers under 25 years of age to 13 large cities all across the United States. These staff members recruited volunteers to hand out leaflets urging people to boycott Schenley products and Delano grapes.

There were two other things about a boycott that Chavez liked. First, it involved lots of people—those encouraging the boycott and those who might be buyers—and it united the union and the consumer. Second, it was nonviolent.

The staff members of the boycott in Boston even came up with the idea for the Boston Grape Party. This was modeled, of course, after the Boston Tea Party of 1773. After marching through the city streets to the waterfront, the marchers gained publicity by tossing Delano grapes into Boston Harbor.

Late in the fall, Chavez decided to concentrate the boycott on Schenley Industries. Grape growing was only a part of the Schenley enterprise. A boycott against all their products, particularly wine (which was made from grapes) and liquor, would be very costly. "I will not buy Schenley products for the duration of the Delano farm workers' strike," read the Schenley boycott pledge. It continued, "Get with it, Schenley, and negotiate. Recognize the National Farm Workers Association." Organizers hoped that even million-dollar advertising budgets would not be able to overcome all the bad publicity Schenley would get.

In December 1965, Walter Reuther of the United Auto Workers (UAW) arrived in Delano. The UAW was one of the strongest unions in the United States. Reuther marched downtown with AWOC and the NFWA. "We will put the full support of organized labor behind your boycott and this is a powerful economic weapon," Walter Reuther said to the assembled strikers. "You are making history here and we will march here together, we will fight here together, and we will win here together."

The United Auto Workers pledged $5,000 a month and the AFL-CIO $10,000 a month to the NFWA. (The AWOC was already receiving money from these two organizations.) But that still left Chavez and his workers far short of what they needed. The strike was already costing the NFWA $40,000 a month. The money was used to help support workers who were not earning wages because they were out on strike.

At a meeting with the mayor of Delano, Reuther said: "Look, you tell the growers that sooner or later these guys [the union] are going to win. I can guarantee you that. . . . Why not talk now and avoid all the bitterness." Before leaving town, Reuther even managed to speak to the growers himself. Although nothing came of that meeting, Reuther's visit had helped push La Causa onto the national stage.

There was another series of events that helped to publicize further the plight of the farm workers. These were the meetings of the U.S. Senate Subcommittee on Migratory Labor held in March 1966. Three days of hearings were scheduled. Hearings are special meetings during which witnesses are heard and information gathered. The first one was in Sacramento. The next one was in San Francisco. And the last one was held right in Delano.

In Delano, Cesar Chavez told the chairperson, Senator Harrison A. Williams of New Jersey, the following:

> Hearings similar to these have been called for decades, and unfortunately things have not changed very much in spite of them. . . . The same exploitation of child labor, the same idea that farm workers are a different breed of people—humble, happy, built close to the ground—prevails.
>
> [T]his generation of farm labor children will not get an adequate education until their parents earn enough to care for the child the way they want to and the way other children in school—the ones who succeed—are cared for.

How this could be achieved was to treat the agricultural workers like all the other workers in the country. Chavez went on to spell out what was needed:

> All we want from the government is the machinery—some rules of the game. All we need is the recognition of our right to full and equal coverage under every law which protects every other working man and woman in this country. What we demand is very simple: we want equality.

Senator Robert F. Kennedy of New York was also a member of this subcommittee. Fortunately, he showed up for the last hearing in Delano. Senator Kennedy questioned Leroy Galyen, the local sheriff, about some recent arrests. The strikebreakers had threatened the strikers, but it was the strikers who were arrested. Senator Kennedy wanted to know why they had been arrested.

"Well, if I have reason to believe that there's going to be a riot started," said the sheriff, "and somebody tells me that there's going to be trouble if you don't stop them, it's my duty to stop them."

63

Chavez speaks to members of the U.S. Senate Subcommittee on Migratory Labor at a hearing in Delano in 1966.

"Who told you that they're going to riot?" Senator Kennedy wanted to know.

"The men [strikebreakers] right out in the field that they [the strikers] were talking to said, 'If you don't get them [the strikers] out of here, we're going to cut their hearts out.' So rather than let them get out, we removed the cause." This was a classic case of blaming the victim for the crime.

Senator Kennedy ended this exchange with the following comment. "Can I suggest that . . . the sheriff and the district attorney read the Constitution of the United States?" The First Amendment, part of the Constitution's Bill of Rights, protects the right to assemble and freedom of speech.

On the very next day, March 17, 1966, Cesar Chavez set out with 67 farm workers on a march from Delano to the state capitol building in Sacramento, about 300 miles away. (In 1930, Mahatma Gandhi, one of Chavez's heroes, had led a 200-mile march to protest British control over India's natural resources.)

The march was in part a protest against Schenley's spraying of NFWA pickets with insecticides. Also, Chavez remembered how well received a march had been in Oxnard. It would be like a *peregrinación*, or pilgrimage, that was so popular in Mexico and often held before Easter. That was why the march would end on Easter Sunday. Some of the marchers who were not Roman Catholic did not like the religious trappings of a pilgrimage. However, after a lengthy discussion, it was decided that the march would be a pilgrimage. That way it would combine a tradition of the Spanish-speaking world with the civil rights march.

The journey's end was Sacramento, the state capital, because state legislators had guaranteed Schenley a minimum price for their liquor. The farm workers disliked the fact that there was a guarantee for the growers when there was no minimum wage for the grape workers.

The march was scheduled to last 25 days. One group of people would go ahead to make arrangements for each day's march. Another group would follow up after the marchers had departed in order to help organize the workers. Along the route it was hoped that people would come out and join the marchers in support of La Causa.

A written plan was drawn up for the occasion. Years before, during the Mexican Revolution, Zapata, another of Chavez's heroes, had issued the Plan of Ayala. The farm workers called theirs the Plan of Delano. The Plan of Delano told of how the farm workers were tired of the way things were and how they were going to elect new leaders in government who would be sympathetic to their cause. The Plan of Delano contained these words designed to inspire action:

> Across the San Joaquin Valley, across California, across the entire southwest of the United States . . . our movement is spreading like flames across a dry plain.

CHAPTER SIX

The Road to Sacramento

There was a problem at the beginning of the 1966 march. The police did not want the marchers to go through downtown Delano. After a three-hour delay, city officials ordered the police to let the marchers pass, and the strikers wound their way out of town onto the highway.

In 1966, Cesar Chavez and striking farm workers marched almost 300 miles from Delano to Sacramento.

At the head of the march, workers carried the flags of the United States, Mexico, the Philippines, the NFWA, and the AWOC. Also, they carried a banner with a picture of Our Lady of Guadalupe, the patron saint of the poor. Following behind in single file were the workers. Many had red hatbands or arm bands with the black Aztec eagle. Some carried AWOC and *huelga* (strike) banners.

Somewhere in the middle walked Cesar Chavez. As he once said: "It is like taking a road over hills and down into the valley: you must stay with the people. If you go ahead too fast, then they lose sight of you and you lose sight of them." Here the metaphor had become reality.

After each day's march, the marchers and the people along the way joined together for a festival. There were speeches and a reading of the Plan of Delano. Guitars and accordions appeared for dancing and singing. There were *corridas*, or ballads, sung about the strike and about their pilgrimage. One such *corrida* was the following, titled "Long Live the General Strike!":

> On the 8th of September
> From the camps of Delano
> Came the Filipinos.
>
> And then after two weeks
> To unite in the battle
> Out came the Chicanos.
> And together we're fulfilling
> The march of history
> To liberate our people.
>
> *Chorus*
> Long live the farm strike!
> Long live our historic cause!
> Our people crowned with glory!
> Will achieve the victory!

There was also a performance presented by El Teatro Campesino, the Farm Workers Theater, dramatizing the struggle between the workers and the growers. The people in the crowd clapped and cheered for the striker. They hissed the grower, who wore a pig mask. They booed "Don Coyote," the farm labor contractor. And before the evening was over, all locked arms and sang "Nosotros Venceremos," the Spanish version of "We Shall Overcome," the anthem of the civil rights movement.

For Cesar Chavez, the march also became a personal pilgrimage. After the first day's march of 21 miles, he had a blistered foot and swollen ankle. (Chavez had been too busy to outfit himself with a good pair of shoes.) After the second day's march of 17 miles, his leg was swollen to the knee. By the fourth day, his leg was swollen to the thigh. By the seventh day, Chavez was trembling with fever. A nurse accompanying the march made him ride for part of the next day. After he began walking again, Chavez used a cane. But he was in pain all the way to Sacramento.

In Fresno, the mayor had lunch prepared for the marchers. In Modesto, many other unions turned out as a sign of support. And in Stockton, 5,000 people greeted the marchers.

There was also a phone call for Chavez. When Chavez finally came to the phone, a voice said he was calling from Schenley. "I want to talk to you about recognizing the Union and signing a contract." Chavez hung up. He didn't have time for any crackpot calls. The phone rang again. People from Schenley Industries wanted to meet with Cesar Chavez the next day in Beverly Hills.

Chris Hartmire of the Migrant Ministry drove a sleeping Cesar Chavez through the California night. At the meeting a preliminary agreement was signed between Schenley and Chavez. Schenley Industries recognized the National Farm Workers Association. It granted an increase of 35 cents to $1.75 an hour. Schenley Industries established a union hall for hiring workers as well as a credit union. The formal signing of the contract would be in June.

When Chavez returned to the marchers to tell them the news, the cheers were long and loud. The excitement rose the closer they came to their destination. All along the way, people joined the march.

Finally, on Easter Sunday, the march arrived in Sacramento. A three-hour rally was held under a light rain on the steps of the

From the steps of the California Capitol in Sacramento, Chavez waves to the supporters of the grape workers' strike.

capitol building. Edmund G. "Pat" Brown, the Democratic governor of California, had left town for a weekend in Palm Springs at the home of Frank Sinatra. However, some other politicians were there. And in the place of honor in the crowd of 10,000 were the original 67 marchers.

The news about Schenley was again greeted enthusiastically. And once more the Plan of Delano was read aloud before the farm workers and the crowd:

> We are tired of words, of betrayals, of indifference. To the politicians we say that the years are gone when the farm worker said nothing and did nothing to help himself. From this movement shall spring leaders who shall understand us, lead us, be faithful to us, and we shall elect them to represent us. We shall be heard!

It seemed that the workers could never hear the conclusion too many times. The Plan of Delano was greeted by the same enthusiastic response on the steps of the California state capitol as it had received all along the way:

> Our Pilgrimage is the match that will light our cause for all farm workers to see what is happening here, that they may do as we have done. . . . History is on our side. May the Strike go on.
> *Viva La Huelga! Viva La Causa!*

As the marchers had been approaching Sacramento, Chavez heard other exciting news: The DiGiorgio Fruit Corporation, the second largest producer of grapes, was willing to hold an election to determine which union the workers wanted to represent them. (DiGiorgio, the owner, had been around a long time. He had even been the basis for Gregorio, a character in John Steinbeck's 1939 prizewinning novel, *The Grapes of Wrath*.) At first, the news sounded good. Then details began to emerge. One was that the replacement workers, not the workers on strike, would be the ones to vote.

A few days after the march, the NFWA stepped up its strike against the DiGiorgio Fruit Corporation. It was not easy to maintain the grape strike. Yet, it was worth it. As Chavez has said: "The picket line is where a man makes his commitment, and it's irrevocable; and the longer he's on the picket line, the stronger the commitment."

DiGiorgio wanted the International Brotherhood of Teamsters to represent the workers. The Teamsters were known for making deals favorable to the growers. For instance, they would sign contracts without even negotiating wages for the workers. To increase the likelihood that the Teamsters would win, DiGiorgio was going to allow only the replacement workers, not the strikers, to vote. To protest these tactics, Chavez had the NFWA removed from the ballot. The NFWA was also encouraging the replacement workers not to vote for the remaining unions on the ballot: the Teamsters and the AWOC.

However, it was hard for the NFWA to speak or get any information to these replacement workers. The strikers and NFWA organizers were not even allowed on the DiGiorgio ranch. Then on May 20, 1966, a court injunction was issued. An injunction is an order not to do something. In this case it was an order that strikers not picket. Then three of the women strikers came up with an idea that would get around the problem of not being able to spread information about the strike demands by means of picketing: Set up a shrine to Our Lady of Guadalupe in the back of Chavez's station wagon.

Over the next two months, the station wagon with the shrine was driven from camp to camp. Wherever it went, day and night, people surrounded the shrine built by Richard Chavez. Whenever workers came over to find out what was going on, strikers handed them leaflets about Chavez's union. The distribution of information was made easier when on June 16 the court overturned the injunction against picketing. Judge Leonard Ginsburg found that DiGiorgio had used violence, the union had not.

On June 21, 1966, the Schenley contract was officially signed with Chavez's union. This was the first real agricultural union contract ever signed in California.

Despite this workers' victory, members of the NFWA had no

time to celebrate. The election to choose a union at DiGiorgio's Sierra Vista Ranch was to be held on June 24. Fewer than half of the farm workers voted in the election. In addition, voting irregularities were discovered. For instance, even some clerks in the DiGiorgio office had voted. Because of such unfair voting practices, Dolores Huerta urged that a new election be held. The unions and the growers submitted the dispute to the American Arbitration Association and agreed to follow its decision. The American Arbitration Association decided that a new, fair election was needed and scheduled it for August 30.

Fred Ross helped to negotiate the rules for the new election. All field hands who were working for DiGiorgio the day before the strike began would be eligible to vote for whichever union they wanted to represent them. Also, union organizers would have the opportunity to talk to the replacement workers on DiGiorgio property at lunchtime and after work.

As the days passed, it seemed that the Teamsters were going to win the new election. NFWA hopes seemed even dimmer when DiGiorgio fired 190 of their workers and replaced them with Anglo high-school students. But Chavez and his *campesinos,* or farm laborers, just worked harder.

Just before the vote, the leaders of the Agricultural Workers Organizing Committee (AWOC) and the National Farm Workers Association (NFWA) realized something important: They had worked well together on the march and since then. Cesar Chavez and Larry Itliong believed it would be more effective for them to combine into one union. Also, this new united union would need to have the formal backing of the AFL-CIO (American Federation of Labor and Congress of Industrial Organizations) in order to compete with the Teamsters. (AWOC had often received money from the AFL-CIO.) So, on August 22, 1966, the United Farm Workers Organizing Committee (UFWOC) was formed. Chavez became the director of the United Farm Workers Organizing Committee. Larry Itliong became its assistant director.

The UFWOC was now a part of a larger labor organization, the AFL-CIO. One of the first things that the AFL-CIO did was to bring in several huge members of the Seafarers International Union to protect the UFWOC. Not surprisingly as a result, the

Teamsters were careful to avoid any physical conflicts with UFWOC strikers.

On August 30, the DiGiorgio workers voted on which union they wanted to represent them. The workers could cast their ballot for the UFWOC, the Teamsters, or no union. On September 2, 1966, the final results were released. In the fields, the vote was 530 for the United Farm Workers Organizing Committee and 331 for the International Brotherhood of Teamsters. In the storage sheds it was a different story: Teamsters, 97; UFWOC, 45. This was the first fair election held among a grower's workers for union representation.

Chavez could breathe a sigh of relief. The UFWOC had won a victory for the field-workers over the Teamsters, the largest and wealthiest union in the world. This had certainly been an important win. "I knew that if we lost this one, we would lose the Union," said Chavez, "because the public wouldn't have supported us after that."

Among the congratulations received by Chavez and his union was this telegram from the Reverend Martin Luther King, Jr.:

> You And Your Valiant Fellow Workers Have Demonstrated Your Commitment To Righting Grievous Wrongs Forced Upon Exploited People. We Are Together With You In Spirit And In Determination That Our Dreams For A Better Tomorrow Will Be Realized.

One of the first things that Chavez did as head of the UFWOC was to end all the contracts with the labor contractors. He knew that many of the AWOC organizers had been making extra money from these contracts. In addition, the AWOC organizers had been making $125 a week. The NFWA organizers, on the other hand, had been making only $5 a week, plus room and board.

Chavez wanted all the organizers to be on an equal basis with the strikers. All organizers would make the same low salary. "If we're going to lead people and ask them to starve and to really sacrifice," declared Chavez, "we've got to do it first."

Chavez also had definite goals for this new union. "We don't want to model ourselves on industrial unions," he said. "We want to get involved in politics, in voter registration, not just contract negotiation. . . . We have to find some cross between being a movement and being a union. The membership must maintain control; the power must not be centered in a few."

From time to time Chavez also journeyed to other states to help other farm workers in their fight. On September 5, 1966, Chavez flew to Texas to join other marchers for the last leg of a 400-mile march from the banks of the Rio Grande to the state capitol in Austin.

Less than two weeks after the election at the DiGiorgio ranch, a crew of grape workers was fired at the Perelli-Minetti ranch near Delano. The workers came to Chavez, who agreed to help them strike. The grower, though, signed a contract with the Teamsters to bring in scab workers. Chavez began a grape boycott to go along with the strike.

Another election was held, this time at the Goldberg ranch in Delano on November 15. One of the questions on the ballot was "Do you want to be represented by the United Farm Workers Organizing Committee?" Out of 377 voters, 285 said yes.

By the end of the year, Cesar Chavez and the UFWOC were able to plan for the future. The union purchased 40 acres of land two miles west of Delano and built the headquarters, which they called Forty Acres. There would be space for a union hiring hall, a credit union, the printing press for *El Malcriado*, and a service center for information on problems such as citizenship and taxes. There would even be a gas station. The goal was to make Forty Acres the headquarters of the UFWOC as well as a cooperative center for migrant workers.

On April 1, 1967, the UFWOC and the DiGiorgio Fruit Corporation signed a contract. It was even better than the one drawn up with Schenley. The new contract also provided for unemployment compensation, a fund for welfare and health benefits, as well as one unpaid day off a week.

Almost a year after the boycott against Perelli-Minetti grapes had begun, the grower was desperate. The boycott had been effective. Chavez met with the Teamsters and the grower. It was decided on July 21, 1967, that the UFWOC would be the union for the field-workers. The Teamsters would be the union for those people who worked in the trucks, the sheds, and the canneries—the factories for canning the food.

However, a very important contract that Chavez and the UFWOC wanted but could not seem to get was one with the Giumarra Vineyards.

CHAPTER SEVEN

The Struggle for Justice

John Giumarra, Sr., had arrived penniless from Sicily in 1920. Soon he was operating a fruit stand in Los Angeles and buying land in California's San Joaquin Valley. The land was not usable until an irrigation system built by the government made the cultivation of grapes possible. Giumarra had gone from rags

Workers load grapes onto a truck. In 1967, Chavez organized a strike and a boycott against California table grapes.

to riches, and he was not about to give anything away. This self-made man was not at all sympathetic to the farm workers' fight.

On August 3, 1967, the UFWOC began another strike against the Giumarra Vineyards. On September 14, Chavez started a boycott of Giumarra, the largest producer of table grapes in the United States.

By the end of 1967 the California table grape boycott included New York City, Boston, Chicago, Detroit, and Los Angeles. John Giumarra was making things difficult by using 100 different labels. It had become impossible to tell which grapes not to buy. Fred Ross and Dolores Huerta came up with the solution. Boycott all California table grapes. However, it was not only a boycott against California table grapes. It was a secondary boycott, too. This meant that the boycott had been expanded to include the chain stores that carried California table grapes. Consumers were being discouraged from doing any shopping at all at these stores.

As time went by, Cesar Chavez was becoming unhappy with how the union was operating. There was more and more talk of using violence. Staff members quarreled among themselves. There was even a growing feeling that everyone in the UFWOC was not working for a common cause. Cesar Chavez wanted to do something that would turn things around and make the members of the union reconsider their priorities. What he decided upon was surprising to many. He began a fast. He stopped eating, only on occasion sipping water. Chavez had read about Mahatma Gandhi's using fasts to draw attention to British oppression in India. Perhaps there was also an element of self-sacrifice in Cesar Chavez. In any case, the fast was another act of nonviolence.

At first, few people knew about Chavez's fast. But as one day stretched into the next, Chavez moved a bed into his office at Forty Acres. He needed to save his strength. Day and night, people came by to wish him well, to talk with him, to get advice. Many set up tents in order to be nearby.

On the twelfth day of the fast, Cesar Chavez had to appear before the California Superior Court in Bakersfield on a charge of contempt of court, that is, disobeying the court. The picketers had not been following a court order. They were not staying 100 yards apart. The picketers were maintaining more than the permitted three picketers at the main entrance of the ranch.

A weakened Chavez was greeted by more than 3,000 farm workers at the courthouse. They remained silent, kneeling on the steps, and lining the halls of the courthouse. Once inside the packed courtroom, the lawyers for Giumarra insisted that the farm workers had to leave. The judge stated that that would be just another form of "gringo justice." (*Gringo* is Spanish slang for a foreigner, especially an American who is white and English-speaking.) The judge would not order the workers to leave. Then he postponed the hearing for two months.

The fast brought people together for the purpose of strengthening the union. Good things—big and small—started to happen. Members of the union discovered things they could accomplish on their own to make the union stronger. Walter Reuther's UAW donated $50,000 to be used for a headquarters building at Forty Acres.

For Chavez, the fast helped him focus on the situation. "I began to see that there were more important things than some of the problems that upset me."

On March 10, 1968, Cesar Chavez ended his fast on the 25th day. He had lost 35 pounds. To celebrate the end of the fast, a mass and demonstration were held that afternoon. Thousands of farm workers marched to a Delano park. Part of the excitement was because of Senator Robert Kennedy's arrival. "[T]he world must know that the migrant farm worker, the Mexican American is coming into his own right," he told the cheering crowd. He said that he had attended that day to show support "for one of the heroic figures of our time—Cesar Chavez." The rest of the excitement was reserved for Chavez.

Exhausted from his ordeal, Chavez had to be helped to his seat between Senator Kennedy and Juana Chavez, his mother. Cesar Chavez was too weak to read his own speech; it was read for him first in Spanish and then in English.

"Our struggle is not easy," read Jim Drake. "Those who oppose our cause are rich and powerful, and they have many allies in high places." (Ronald Reagan, who later became President of the United States, was one. During his successful campaign for governor of California in 1966, Reagan had spoken

Cesar Chavez with Senator Robert Kennedy at the March 1968 demonstration celebrating the end of Chavez's fast.

out repeatedly against the grape strike.) "We are poor," continued the staff member from Migrant Ministry. "Our allies are few. But we have something the rich do not own. We have our own bodies and spirits and the justice of our cause as our weapons."

"When we are really honest with ourselves," read Drake to the quiet crowd, "we must admit that our lives are all that really belong to us. So it is how we use our lives that determines what kind of men we are. It is my deepest belief that only by giving our lives do we find life."

Cesar Chavez remained motionless, his eyes closed, as his concluding words were read: "I am convinced that the truest act of courage . . . is to sacrifice ourselves for others in a totally non-violent struggle for justice." These words would soon be tested. On April 4, 1968, Martin Luther King, Jr., was assassinated. Chavez wrote the following in a telegram to King's widow, Coretta Scott King: "DESPITE THE TRAGIC VIOLENCE THAT TOOK YOUR HUSBAND, THERE IS MUCH THAT IS GOOD ABOUT OUR NATION. IT WAS TO THAT GOODNESS THAT YOUR HUSBAND APPEALED."

Six days after Senator Robert Kennedy's appearance at the mass, he announced that he was seeking the Democratic nomination for United States president. Cesar Chavez went to work helping to get out the Chicano vote. He saw a Kennedy presidency as a good thing for the farm worker and the country. As Senator Kennedy had stated earlier, "[T]he world must know that the migrant farm worker, the Mexican American is coming into his own right."

The high percentage of Chicano votes for Kennedy was a major reason why the senator from New York won the California primary. Hours after this high point came the lowest point imaginable. On the night of the primary election, June 5, 1968, Senator Robert F. Kennedy was assassinated.

It was a difficult time for the country, for the principles of nonviolence, and for Chavez. "Kennedy was by far the real force for change," said Chavez, "and he was willing to take in the poor and make the poor part of his campaign. It [the assassination] was a tremendous setback."

As time went on, the violence around the ranches increased. On July 2, 1968, a truck driver drove into a crowd of picketers.

William Joseph Richardson, a 22-year-old seminary student from Indiana, was injured. Not surprisingly, some of the strikers started to hit back.

Chavez felt it was time to make a change. He shifted the emphasis from the strike and intensified the boycott. People who had been on the picket line now went to major cities to help spread the word about the boycott.

The boycott was having an effect in certain cities. In New York City, for example, only 200 boxcars of grapes had been shipped over a three-month period. A year earlier, over 1,000 boxcars of grapes had been shipped over the same period of time. Overall, however, grape sales had not decreased. Much of the reason lay with the U.S. Department of Defense. The military was shipping abroad tons of table grapes for the soldiers in Vietnam. "This amounts to about 8 pounds a day for each American serviceman in Vietnam," Chavez told an audience at the Walter P. Reuther Auditorium in Detroit. "If a soldier is sick one day, the next day he must eat 16 pounds." It was a bitter joke that Chavez told.

During the fall of 1968, Chavez was undergoing physical pain of his own. His back started giving him so much trouble that he was confined to bed for weeks at a time. Chavez may have been paying the price for years of stoop labor. He would just have to learn to live with it.

Several leading politicians were not among the many people who supported Chavez and his farm workers. Ronald Reagan, the Republican governor of California, and Richard Nixon, the soon-to-be-elected Republican President of the United States, were photographed together eating grapes. And a Republican senator from California, George Murphy, said that the UFWOC claims of pesticide poisoning were merely to "harass the grape industry."

Senator Murphy's claim contradicted the government. An official of the U.S. Food and Drug Administration stated that throughout the United States there were 80,000 pesticide injuries and 800 deaths each year. This only added to the difficulty of the life of the farm workers. Their life expectancy was only 49 years. Nationwide at that time, people on average could expect to live to be over 70.

One thing that pained Chavez as much as anything was any

suggestion that his union was violent. But the president of the California Grape and Tree Fruit League claimed just that. He accused Chavez of using violent tactics. Cesar Chavez answered that charge in what is now known as the Good Friday Letter of April 1969.

> Dear Mr. Barr:
>
> I am sad to hear about your accusations in the press that our union movement and table grape boycott have been successful because we have used violence and terror tactics. If what you say is true, I have been a failure and should withdraw from the struggle.
>
> . . . By lying about the nature of our movement, Mr. Barr, you are working against non-violent social change.
>
> We are men and women who have suffered and endured much and not only because of our abject poverty but because we have been kept poor. . . . But God knows that we are not beasts of burden, we are not agricultural implements or rented slaves, we are men.

In his letter, Chavez was making the point that he and his union did not hate the growers. However, it was necessary for agribusiness to recognize that they were dealing with people.

One of the many ways that the growers treated the farm workers as less than people was by forcing them to use the short-handle hoe. "I think this is where the employer shows the most contempt for his workers," declared Chavez. "All that stooping is one reason farm workers die before they're fifty."

In 1969, the union learned that there was another kind of contract affecting their leader. Someone had put up $25,000 to kill Chavez. Chavez was given a German shepherd by a newspaperman. Named Boycott, the guard dog became a constant companion. "I never thought I could like a dog so much," said Chavez. Even so, security measures were further tightened. Another German shepherd was added. The new dog was named Huelga. Chavez's office was moved to a more secure location. It was a difficult time for Cesar Chavez and the UFWOC. Chavez did not like to feel like a prisoner. Still, he realized it was pointless to endanger his life.

One person who had learned the power of nonviolence was Fernando Chavez, Helen and Cesar Chavez's oldest son. Because of his belief in nonviolence, Fernando had claimed conscientious objector status. Conscientious objectors are people who refuse to serve in the armed forces because of moral or religious principles. At that time, young men were being drafted into the armed forces to fight in Vietnam. Fernando Chavez's draft board, however, refused to classify him as a C.O. So on April 23, 1969, at the height of the Vietnam War, Fernando refused to be inducted into the army at the Fresno induction center. His case would not be decided for two years.

"The decision that Polly [Fernando's nickname] has made and his reasons for it are his own," said Cesar Chavez about his son. "But it is a decision that I very much agree with. A year ago, during my fast for nonviolence, I said that if to build our union would require the deliberate taking of life, either the life of a grower or his child, then I would choose not to see our union built. Today Polly has chosen to respect life and not kill in war. Such a decision is not easy to make and my heart goes out to all parents and children who are faced with a similar challenge of nonviolence."

Almost five years after the grape strike had begun, three growers signed contracts with the UFWOC in April 1970. The terms were $1.75 an hour and 25 cents a box. Just as promising was the fact that these growers also banned six pesticides, including DDT. Lionel Steinberg was one of these growers. After a year of negotiations, he had signed a contract on April 2, 1970. Steinberg had signed because he realized how effective the boycott had been. In Steinberg's words, it had been a "social, political boycott . . . unparalleled in American history."

The Schenley, DiGiorgio, and Steinberg contracts were just the beginning. In the next three months, almost every grower in the Coachella Valley signed a contract. By July, four out of every five grape-growing acres in California were under contract with the UFWOC. The growers around Delano, however, continued to resist.

Chavez celebrates the signing of contracts between the UFWOC and the California grape growers in 1970.

But by July 17, there were 23 growers ready to sit down and talk. Catholic bishops helped the two sides to get together at a motel in Bakersfield and start negotiating.

Then early in the morning on July 26, 1970, Chavez was telephoned by Jerry Cohen, the union lawyer. John Giumarra, Sr., wanted to talk. Chavez suggested the next day. "No, he wants to talk now," said the union lawyer. Two leading chain stores had refused to stock Giumarra's grapes. That meant there would soon be nowhere in the country where he could sell his grapes.

The meeting began in a room at the Stardust Motel in Delano after one o'clock in the morning. Giumarra, a man in his late 60s, and Chavez, 43 years old, sat down and began to talk. The talk lasted through the night and into the next day. It didn't stop until nine in the morning. Then it began again at noon at a nearby Catholic school. On one side of the table were the growers, and on the other was the workers' negotiation committee. By Monday night the lawyers for both sides had taken over. And on Wednesday, July 23, 1970, all the details had been settled and the contract was ready for signing. Instead of his customary plaid sport shirt, Chavez wore an embroidered white Filipino shirt for the ceremony, perhaps highlighting the importance of the old AWOC union in the success of the UFWOC.

The contract established an hourly wage of $1.80, which would increase to $2.05 in 1972. There would be a union hiring hall and money set aside by the employer for workers' benefits. Ten cents an hour would go to the Robert F. Kennedy Health and Welfare Fund. Two cents a box would go to the economic development fund. Also, there would be more precautions taken against the danger of pesticides. After five years, the grape strike and boycott were finally over.

CHAPTER EIGHT

"They Can Never Jail the Cause"

But there was no time to rest. The Teamsters, the other union in the Salinas Valley, were taking over the lettuce industry. The Teamsters were signing contracts with the lettuce growers up and down the valley. This was in violation of the 1967 agreement. In that year the two unions had agreed that the UFWOC would sign up the field-workers. The Teamsters would control the workers in the sheds, canneries, and trucks. To make matters even worse, the Teamsters signed a contract with a grower without negotiating wages for the farm workers. It was a grower's contract. Naturally, UFWOC organizers considered the Teamsters to be a union on the side of the growers.

Although they had just ended the five-year table-grape strike and boycott, Chavez's union began a strike to improve the conditions for lettuce workers. The Teamsters brought in thugs to intimidate the UFWOC, harassing strikers on the picket lines with threats, chains, and baseball bats. Sometimes they even beat up the strikers.

When a judge ordered his union to stop picketing, Chavez began a fast in protest. After a few days, however, he had to stop. His health was too fragile to continue. In fact, Chavez had to get away for a complete rest in order to restore his health.

Another difficult situation in the summer of 1970 was the rise of Chicano power. Mexican-American youths were protesting the high number of Chicanos fighting in Vietnam, while here at home their living conditions were inferior. Chavez certainly understood their feelings. He had even had his own *pachuco* days when a youth. But he did not want the growing cry for brown power to spill over into cries for *La Raza*, meaning "the race" or "our people." Some supporters of *La Raza* promoted their own Mexican background and culture as superior to others. Chavez felt about one culture compared to another in the same way as he regarded religion. "To me, religion is a most beautiful thing," Chavez said. "And over the years, I have come to realize that all religions are beautiful. Your religion just happens to depend a lot on your upbringing and your culture."

On August 24, 1970, about 2,000 workers went out on strike in Salinas. On the second day of the strike, Jerry Cohen was visiting a ranch to check out a sit-down strike among broccoli workers. While he was on the grower's property, a thug from the Teamsters attacked him. Jerry Cohen suffered head injuries and had to be hospitalized.

By the third day, there were 10,000 workers on strike. It was the biggest farm worker strike in U.S. history. But what bothered the United Fruit Company even more was the threat of a boycott. By the seventh day of the strike, August 31, 1970, Dolores Huerta managed to get a contract with Inter Harvest, a major grower of lettuce owned by the United Fruit Company. The terms raised the hourly wage from $1.75 to $2.10. The Teamsters' contract had only called for $1.85.

This poster urges people to boycott lettuce and grapes.

The other lettuce growers rebelled against this contract. They convinced the Teamsters not to use their trucks to move the lettuce from the fields to the cooling plants. The lettuce crop spoiled in the hot sun. To help avoid violence from the Teamsters, the AFL-CIO called in tough members of the Seafarers union as they had in 1966.

The strike and boycott that were once directed against grapes Chavez had now shifted to lettuce. By the end of August, the strikers were picketing 40 lettuce growers in Salinas Valley. The strike was spreading. Even more damaging would be the boycott to be carried out in 64 cities. As had happened earlier with the grape strike, there was the problem of boycotting only a few growers. The UFWOC decided to boycott all brands associated with lettuce, except those of Inter Harvest and the United Fruit Company.

Another problem had also occurred before. The California Superior Court ordered a permanent injunction not to picket Bud Antle, the owner of the largest lettuce farm. As he had done during the grape strike, Chavez refused to obey the court. Again, he knew that if the UFWOC followed orders, the strike would lose its effectiveness. Without picketing, the strike and boycott would create less pressure for the growers to change.

In the fall of 1970, District Court Judge Gordon Campbell ordered Cesar Chavez to call off the lettuce boycott. Chavez, however, refused. So on December 4, 1970, Cesar Chavez was required to appear in court.

To show their support of Chavez, more than 2,000 farm workers marched to the courthouse in Salinas. After their arrival, they stood silently for hours in and around the courthouse. Inside the courtroom, Judge Gordon Campbell listened to both sides argue their case. When they were through, the judge exited the courtroom for his chambers. Only ten minutes later, he returned and read a long typewritten ruling:

> If the law is to continue to have any meaning, it must continue to apply equally to the weak and the strong, to the poor and the rich, favoring neither the one nor the other. . . . If the objective is a noble objective—and many say there is a noble objective here—improper and evil methods cannot be permitted to justify it.

After finishing the reading of his judgment, Judge Campbell then sentenced Chavez to jail for contempt of court. The union leader was to remain in jail until he called off the boycott.

Before leaving the courtroom, Judge Gordon Campbell imposed a $10,000 fine. Bill Carder, Chavez's lawyer, objected

Although Chavez refused to obey court orders against picketing lettuce growers, he asked picketers "to be peaceful."

because the fine was too much. The judge realized that the lawyer was right. Quickly, he reduced the fine to $1,000—$500 for each count of contempt of court—and hurried from the courtroom.

Cesar Chavez was taken to jail. Coretta Scott King, the widow of Martin Luther King, Jr., visited him in jail. So did Ethel Kennedy, the widow of Robert F. Kennedy. Chavez stayed busy. He planned out every hour and even counseled other prisoners. "There was a time for meditation, a time for reading, a time for my mail, a time for exercise, a time for planning, and times to wash up and shave and clean up."

Outside the Salinas jail, farm workers waited 24 hours a day. They vowed to stay there until Chavez was released. That time came after 20 days. On Christmas Eve, Chavez walked out of jail. The California Supreme Court had ordered Chavez released while they reviewed his case. "My spirit was never in jail," stated Chavez. "They can jail us, but they can never jail the Cause."

Four months later, the California Supreme Court overturned the lower court's injunction. The California Supreme Court had ruled it was unconstitutional. Consequently, the case was dropped. It was quite legal for the UFWOC to boycott Bud Antle.

Victory in the fields, however, did not come as quickly. The talks between the growers and the UFWOC dragged on and on. Frustrated, Chavez broke off the talks in November 1971. Still, Cesar Chavez was able to take a long-range view. He understood why agribusiness was so threatened by a union of farm workers: Chavez's union stood for political changes not just for higher wages and better working conditions.

"They knew that once our Movement wins, it's going to have concrete power in terms of workers, in terms of things it can do for people. And they know it's not going to stop there," declared Chavez. "They know that in a few years farm workers will be sitting on city councils, county boards, and the courts. That's where the Movement is going to lead us."

91

CHAPTER NINE

A Life of Nonviolence

Cesar Chavez was beginning to be recognized for his hard work and accomplishments. Chavez's policy was that if things were not going well, he would just work harder. Another policy of his was that he would not accept any awards for his own work. When the Society for the Family of Man tried to give him the 1970 Human Relations Award, Chavez turned it down. "[T]he struggle is not mine," he stated, "but that of thousands of farm workers."

Working conditions on farms affected not only adults. In 1970, the American Friends Service Committee released an important report. It stated that "the agricultural child labor scene in 1970 is reminiscent of the sweatshop scene in 1938." They discovered six-year-old children working 8 to 10 hours in the fields. In one county in Maine, children were responsible for bringing in 35 percent of the potato crop.

Many times it was hard to stick to a life of nonviolence. However, there were personal victories along the way. On August 12, 1971, the charges against Fernando Chavez for refusing to be inducted into the armed forces were dropped. A federal court judge in Fresno, California, had concluded that there could be more than just religious beliefs to qualify a person as a conscientious objector.

That same year, the UFWOC called a halt to the lettuce boycott for five months because the growers insisted that it would help negotiations. However, the talks between the union and the lettuce growers still did not get anywhere. On November 10, 1971, the talks ground to a halt.

However, talks were going smoothly somewhere else. In February 1972, Manuel Chavez led negotiations in Florida to success. A union contract was signed with Coca-Cola to cover migrant workers in Coca-Cola's citrus groves. It was the first union contract covering migrant workers in the state of Florida.

Also in February 1972, the AFL-CIO gave a national charter to Chavez's union. The UFWOC was now an official part of the AFL-CIO, one of the most important labor organizations in the country. This union of 30,000 farm workers changed its name, too. From now on it would be known as the United Farm Workers, or the UFW.

Chavez and the United Farm Workers had not only the International Brotherhood of Teamsters, the world's largest union, against them. The American Farm Bureau Federation, the powerful growers' association, also opposed them. And to top it off, the administration of President Richard M. Nixon in Washington, D.C., permitted the Defense Department to be the biggest buyer of grapes and lettuce. Opposition to Chavez ranged from the local grower to the President of the United States. "Because we were dealing with a national campaign against us, we wanted to have a showdown and Arizona became the best place, other than California, to have it," reasoned Chavez.

Most of the previous effort of the UFW had been in California. But in May 1972, the neighboring state of Arizona became the focus of union activity. Arizona's Republican governor, Jack Williams, had quickly signed a bill sponsored by the American Farm Bureau, favorable to the growers. This bill not only outlawed strikes and boycotts but also made it difficult for migrant workers to vote in elections for unions. When farm workers tried to arrange a meeting with the governor, Williams replied, "As far as I'm concerned, these people do not exist."

"Somehow," said Chavez, "these powerful men and women must be helped to realize that there is nothing to fear from treating their workers as fellow human beings."

The union started a campaign to collect signatures to recall the governor. (A recall is a special election in which the people can vote to remove an elected official from office.) They also began a drive to register Chicanos, Native Americans, and poor people to vote. The recall of the governor might have once seemed impossible, but now it had become possible. At meetings the battle cry of "Si se puede!" ("Yes, it's possible!") rang out.

Cesar Chavez began another fast on May 11, 1972. From a bed at a community center in Phoenix, Arizona, he directed the union's activity. Again, he fasted to point out the importance of nonviolence. As Chavez once wrote (echoing a warning of Gandhi's): "[F]asting is the last resort in place of the sword." Chavez believed that by fasting he communicated his position more swiftly than regular publicity. "It's not done out of a desire to destroy myself," Chavez said, "but it's done out of a deep conviction that we can communicate to people, either those who are for us or against us."

Even so, the fast was a painful one for Chavez. It also caused real concern for Chavez's health. His heartbeat was irregular, and the level of uric acid in his system became very high. Chavez had to be hospitalized until his condition became more stable. By the time the fast was over on the 24th day, many people sympathetic to La Causa had visited Cesar Chavez. Among them were Senator George McGovern, the Democratic nominee for President of the United States. Others were Joseph Kennedy (the son of Robert Kennedy and today a member of the House of Representatives from Massachusetts), the famous folksinger Joan Baez, and Coretta Scott King.

In all, 108,000 valid signatures had been collected to recall the Arizona governor. This was 5,000 more than was needed for the recall. However, by the time it had been announced as official, it was too late to hold a special election to recall Jack Williams as governor.

More long-lasting was the effect of the voter registration drive on future Arizona politics. Mexican Americans and Navajos started winning important elections. In 1974, Alfredo Gutierrez became the majority leader of the state senate, and Raul Castro was elected governor of the state.

The next battleground was back in Delano, California, at the end of June 1972. The first contracts that Chavez's union had ever signed had expired. No longer was the Sierra Vista Ranch owned by DiGiorgio. Now, it was called the White River Farms, and the new owner was Buttes Gas and Oil.

Hoping to ease negotiations for a new contract, Chavez offered to share the operation of the hiring hall with the new owners. Both owner and union would be involved with the hiring of workers. Even with this concession, however, Buttes would still not sign a new contract. So finally on September 25, 1972, the United Farm Workers went out on strike.

Strikers were arrested trying to prevent new workers from being bused in to the vineyards. The strikebreakers, on the other hand, were not able to pick enough grapes in time. It proved to be a costly harvest for both sides. Buttes Gas and Oil lost a million dollars. The UFW had lost one of their very first contracts and had been unable to sign a new one.

Typically, Chavez's reaction was even tempered. "This means we won't have contracts for a while," he said. "But we won't dry up and fly away. The workers aren't going to stand by and let them return to the feudal days of labor contractors. . . . [W]e have to keep in touch with the workers to keep their support." But for a while, "everything is going to go to the Teamsters."

And that is exactly what happened. The Teamsters seemed to do whatever it took to win. If they needed to sign authorization cards unlawfully to show workers' support for their union, they would do it. If they needed to truck in hired hoodlums to intimidate strikers, they would do that, too.

But even more disturbing was the fact that the Nixon White House was doing whatever it could to help the Teamsters. Chuck Colson, the chief counsel to the President, made just this point in a 1972 memo to President Richard M. Nixon: "The Teamsters Union is now organizing in the area and will probably sign up most of the grape growers this coming spring and they will need our support against the UFW."

As an American troublemaker, Cesar Chavez had reached the mountaintop. Not only had he battled Ronald Reagan, the governor of California, he was now up against Richard Nixon, the President of the United States. Why would the government be taking sides like this? One reason was that the Teamsters had contributed a lot of money to the Nixon presidential campaign. Nixon was paying back the favor. Another was that Nixon had always sided with the growers against the farm workers.

Certainly this did not come as shocking news to Cesar Chavez, who said of the President:

Because of Nixon's background, we weren't surprised he was against us. He'd been harassing farm worker organizations since the late forties when, as a congressman, he took on the DiGiorgio strikers. He had the full power of subpoena and investigation, and he cross-examined those poor farm workers, eating them up alive. He's an evil man. When he ran for president in 1968, he was the only politician to eat grapes publicly, stuffing himself with grapes before cameras in Fresno.

Chavez called for another lettuce strike in 1973, but it did not change anything. The growers and Teamsters could not be budged. It had not even helped when the California Supreme Court the previous December made a ruling against the growers. The court said that the growers had shown "the ultimate form of favoritism, completely substituting the employer's choice of unions for his employees' desires." In other words, the growers had made so-called sweetheart contracts with the Teamsters. Even so, the UFW was not able to win any more contracts.

The UFW contracts with the grape growers in the Coachella Valley expired in the middle of April 1973. The large majority of farm workers were in favor of renewing contracts with the United Farm Workers. However, most of the growers signed with the Teamsters without consulting the workers.

Teamsters' contracts established a salary of $2.30 per hour for the farm workers but provided little else. There was no hiring hall. There was no set way to handle problems between the workers and the growers. And there was nothing about the control of harmful pesticides.

The day after the contracts were signed, there were more than 1,000 farm workers picketing the growers. The UFW went out on strike, and the Teamsters' hoodlums moved in to protect the strikebreakers. There were many outbreaks of violence, but Cesar Chavez cautioned his picketers not to react violently. "The whole idea of nonviolence is you are not afraid," he said. "If you become afraid you start doing things you are not supposed to do. Violence is a trap."

The courts started issuing orders restricting the activity of the picketers. The UFW was supposed to limit the number of picketers and widen the distance between them. Chavez realized that if the UFW honored these court orders, the strike might as well be over. It would be too ineffective to make a difference.

Chavez warned the strikers of the dangers they would be facing. There would be hired thugs from the Teamsters to threaten them. The police would probably arrest them and take them to jail. Did the strikers still want to march on the picket line? Their answer was "*Si! Huelga!*"

As the picketers arrived, the police moved in and arrested them. They dragged the workers to the waiting vans and off to jail. In a short time, more than 100 strikers had been arrested, including 22-year-old Linda Chavez.

That evening the judge came to the jail to tell the workers they would be arraigned in court in a week's time. This meant that they would have to return to court to answer an indictment, or charge. However, there had been no preliminary hearing. This was in violation of the United States Constitution. When Jerry Cohen, the lawyer for the UFW, tried to advise the workers of their rights, the judge silenced him. This was in violation of their constitutional rights, too. And, of course, the fact they were not allowed to picket in the first place could also be viewed as a violation of freedom of speech under the First Amendment.

Judge Fred Metheny realized the errors of his position. And later when he visited one of the ranches, he saw Teamsters walking around with bats. Judge Fred Metheny changed the injunction to allow picketing 60 feet from the boundary line. In addition, he added that "no person shall try to prevent workers or pickets from entering or leaving the fields with the use of guns, knives, clubs, baseball bats, grape stakes, or other dangerous instruments."

Five months later, there had been over 3,800 arrests in Fresno, Kern, Riverside, and Tulare counties. Over 300 people were seriously injured. But the spirit of the strikers remained high. More than once, arrested strikers refused to walk out of jail unless all the strikers were released.

The hardest thing to deal with, though, was the violence. Strikers were beaten by the Teamsters and even maced and roughed up by the police. Sometimes the strikers fought back. Chavez pleaded with the strike captains to help the strikers realize that they needed to show more discipline. In order to succeed, Chavez reminded them, the strike must remain nonviolent.

Then on a night in August 1973, a deputy police officer hit one of the UFW strike captains on the head with a flashlight. The man fell to the sidewalk in Delano and lay still. Without ever regaining consciousness, Nagi Daifullah from Yemen died the next day.

The day after Daifullah's death, 60-year-old Juan de la Cruz stepped off the picket line to speak to his wife. A bullet fired from a speeding pickup truck struck him in the chest. A few hours later, Cruz died.

Thousands of farm workers turned out for both funerals. Each of the farm workers in the long funeral processions wore a black arm band. "It must be a time to think again about violence and nonviolence," said Chavez. It was a somber time.

Cesar Chavez decided to call off the grape strike. In its place there would be a boycott of California grapes.

Chavez and the UFW needed to take stock of their situation. A constitutional convention was held in San Francisco. Every line of this United Farm Workers' document was reevaluated. It was an education for all the delegates. Perhaps another sign of an education in how to build a democratic union was that for the first time some members were publicly criticizing Chavez. They felt that after the grape strike had ended in 1970 the contracts should have been signed with the growers around Delano. Only after they had signed those contracts should their union have started the strike against the lettuce growers in the Salinas Valley.

At the beginning of September 1973, about 500 farm workers traveled to different cities across the country to help the boycott. Also in September, the UFW and the Teamsters were again talking about which groups they would represent. The two unions decided that the Teamsters would represent the packers, canners, and farm truck drivers. The UFW would represent the fieldworkers. So when 30 growers from the Delano area signed contracts with the Teamsters, Teamster president Frank Fitzsimmons overturned the contracts. But then in November 1973 he changed

Cesar Chavez speaks at the funeral of one of the UFW members killed during the 1973 grape workers' strike.

99

his mind and said there had been no oral agreement with the UFW. (There was a rumor that the Nixon White House had forced this decision.) The two union leaders were as far apart in their thinking as they were in their yearly salaries. Fitzsimmons made $125,000, Chavez only $5,000.

Nevertheless, it was not surprising that people were becoming increasingly unhappy with how the United Farm Workers was being run. The UFW had held over 300 contracts with growers in 1973. A year later they had only a dozen. The Teamsters, on the other hand, held over 350 contracts in 1974.

The UFW membership was down as well. In 1972, the UFW had 60,000 members. Two years later, in 1974, there were only 5,000. In the same year, 55,000 field-workers were members of the Teamsters. The financial situation was no better. The Teamsters were able to spend $100,000 a month on their farm labor operation. At UFW headquarters, Cesar Chavez worried about how to pay for simple office supplies.

For many of the new members of the Teamsters, Cesar Chavez was still their hero. But in their practical workaday world, the Teamsters were now simply offering them a better deal. The wages of members of both unions were about the same: $2.50 an hour. But the Teamsters were starting to provide benefits. There was medical insurance and a pension plan. The Teamsters also provided social workers in the field to help eliminate illegal practices by the labor contractors, improve housing conditions, even assist in filing income taxes.

While the grape boycott stretched into 1974, Chavez relearned two lessons that he had forgotten. "We've got to do exactly what we did back in 1962, 1963, 1964. We must go back to the origins of the Union and do service-center work. The contracts are no substitute for the basic help we provide workers in all aspects of their lives."

The second thing Chavez relearned is that the power comes from the people. Every day presents an opportunity to learn from the workers. "What happens is that in most unions and most societies—be it the church, politics, or whatever," pointed out Chavez, "there is a tremendous pull away from people into paper work and into direction at the top away from the people."

Chavez in 1974. As membership in the UFW fell, he demanded
that California provide a "Bill of Rights for farm workers."

On the other hand, William Grami, the director of the Teamster agricultural organizing project, pointed out:

> The farm workers have been exploited by the growers. They need effective representation. Chavez can't provide that. He's a clever, charismatic, revolutionary leader, but his organization isn't strong enough to deliver. We have no charismatic heroes among Teamster leaders. But we can deliver.

Chavez looked at it differently. He took a long-range view:

> We will not give up. We will not go away. We have been wiped out before. We have been wiped out by the growers, by the courts, by the cops. We have been wiped out every day of our lives—by the short hoe, by the work of the day and the exhaustion of the night. We are very experienced in this business of getting wiped out. The Teamsters can't wipe us out. We will win.

More and more Chavez began to see it was necessary to have a "Bill of Rights for farm workers." With the election of a new governor of California in 1974, Edmund G. (Jerry) Brown, Jr., a California Bill of Rights for farm workers had become possible. It was Governor Jerry Brown who outlawed *el cortito*, the short hoe, in 1975. As Cesar Chavez had once remarked: "*El cortito*, the short hoe . . . [is] the most vicious exploitation of the human body. For a person to bend down for 10 hours a day, to do that work, it's—well, in 10 years the body is just a wreck."

Governor Brown encouraged the growers, the Teamsters, the American Farm Bureau Federation, and Cesar Chavez to begin discussions. One of the biggest helps was the fact that the governor was so well informed and interested.

"Governor Brown was very different from most politicians. He knew changes had to be made," said Chavez. "He was looking for the areas where they should be made. . . . for ways of bringing about meaningful changes, not just cosmetic ones."

After a lot of bargaining and talking back and forth, the groups reached agreement. The bill set forth secret-ballot elections at the peak of the harvest so that the largest number of migrant workers would be able to vote for the union they wanted to represent them. It also stated that growers could not fire workers for supporting a particular union. There would be a board to hear farm workers' grievances, and contracts would be binding for both parties. The new bill would also benefit growers. Unions would not be allowed to use the secondary boycott as they had before.

The California legislature approved the bill, and so the Agricultural Labor Relations Act of 1975 became California law. Migrant workers now had a California Bill of Rights for farm workers.

CHAPTER TEN

A Protector of the Environment

The Agricultural Labor Relations Act of 1975 established a five-member board. Unfortunately, the California Senate in Sacramento withheld money so that the Agricultural Labor Relations Board (ALRB) could not function properly.

To prevent this from happening again, Cesar Chavez backed something called Proposition 14. If passed by the voters of the state, there would be two parts to this law. The first would provide enough money so that the ALRB could operate. The second part of the proposed law would allow union members to go onto growers' property in order to organize their farm workers.

Proposition 14 was voted down by a large majority at an election in November 1976. It was said at the time that if Chavez had just tried to get the funding for the ALRB, "Prop 14" would have passed. What defeated the bill was the section that would have allowed union members onto the property of ranchers. The growers lobbied hard against it and persuaded many voters to vote no.

(More recently, in 1992, the Supreme Court made a ruling concerning the National Labor Relations Board. The Supreme Court's 6-3 decision was written by Justice Clarence Thomas. The Court stated that by allowing union organizers into areas such as employer parking lots, the NLRB had not adequately protected the private property rights of the employer. This case is known as *Lechmere* v. *National Labor Relations Board*, 1991. It will make it more difficult for union organizers, including the UFW organizers, to have direct contact with workers in any of the 50 states. Instead, they will have to settle for less effective methods, such as advertising in local newspapers.)

Another issue that Cesar Chavez became involved in was whether or not illegal aliens should be covered under the NLRB. Chavez believed they should not be. More and more undocumented Mexican workers were illegally entering the United States from Mexico. Chavez saw this as similar to the bracero program he had fought against earlier. Chavez thought there were already enough legal farm workers in this country. These people should get the jobs.

In March 1977, the UFW received some good news. The battle between the Teamsters and the UFW had ended. The Teamsters and the UFW signed a five-year truce for 13 western states. The two unions came to terms along the lines of their original agreement. The Teamsters would get the canners, packers, and farm truck drivers. The UFW would represent the field hands.

Why had the Teamsters given up a fight they had been winning? This seems even more surprising when the resources of the two unions are compared. Even the headquarters of these two unions present a vivid illustration of this difference.

The headquarters of the International Brotherhood of Teamsters faces the U.S. Capitol Building in Washington, D.C. In contrast, the UFW headquarters is located on an isolated rocky stretch of the Tehachapi Mountains high over the California desert. (The UFW had moved its headquarters from Delano in 1971.) The Teamsters building is made of gleaming stone. The UFW headquarters, on the other hand, is a ramshackle collection of old buildings, hospital wings, and cottages. (Given to the UFW by a Hollywood producer, it is a former tuberculosis sanitarium. As a child, Helen Chavez had been a patient there.) This 300-acre area in the mountains has since been renamed La Paz, which means "Peace" or "The Peaceful Place."

The real reason for the "peace treaty" between the two unions had to do with public relations. The Teamsters were under attack for scandals involving their pension funds. They did not need to be struggling with Cesar Chavez as well. Too many people still considered Chavez to be a hero. Besides, people tend to side with the "little guy," with David, rather than with the powerful side, Goliath.

All of a sudden the future looked considerably brighter for Cesar Chavez and the UFW. After a low of 5,000 members in 1974, the membership had increased to 18,000 in 1977. The agreement with the Teamsters resulted in thousands of new members for the UFW. "Now the battle starts with the real opponents—the growers," said Chavez. In 1978, Cesar Chavez called a halt to the grape boycott begun in 1973. Bargaining began in earnest with the growers in the Delano area. After three months, agreements were reached with seven growers.

In 1979, the UFW began a lettuce strike in the Imperial Valley. During the year, Chavez both fasted and led a march to Salinas. In spite of these efforts the strike was bloody and costly. One striker was killed. The growers lost $10 million worth of lettuce. After almost a year, the UFW and several of the growers sat down together to sign contracts.

But elections for union representation continued to be a problem. In 1979, thugs connected with the M. Carratan Company broke up an election for union representation being held at a grape ranch near Delano. They terrorized farm workers and beat up a state agent. They overturned voting booths and even stole the ballot box. The state found the company guilty of violence and ordered them to sign with the UFW. The company refused.

In September 1983, Rene Lopez was shot and killed by a company agent of the Sikkema Dairy Farm where Lopez worked. Lopez had just voted for the UFW in a state-supervised election. "Rene Lopez's death, as well as the deaths of the other martyrs in the union," said Chavez, "shows to what extent the growers will go to keep the workers from having the freedom to decide for themselves whether or not they want to have a union."

Chavez saw one of the problems as a deep-seated attitude among the growers. "It's a way of being, a way of thinking, a way of acting that no one is going to tell them what to do," said Chavez. "The workers get killed, get pressured, get blacklisted, get attacked physically because they want a union."

Another problem that disturbed Chavez was that it seemed that the California state government under Governor George Deukmejian was not even pretending to enforce the laws. "The laws that protect workers are on the books," said Chavez. "But they're not enforced."

The 1980s presented more problems to Cesar Chavez with fewer solutions. Ronald Reagan, who served as President of the

In 1979, Chavez led a protest against lettuce growers. He accused them of hiring Mexicans as illegal strikebreakers.

United States from 1981 to 1989, was hostile to Cesar Chavez and the UFW. But the hostility toward Chavez also came from some members of his own union.

Many members did not like the powerful role that Cesar Chavez continued to hold in the union. They also did not like being encouraged to try meditation and vegetarianism. (It is not difficult to understand Chavez's enthusiasm for vegetarianism. Chavez had back problems until he changed his diet.) Nor did they appreciate Chavez's interest in holistic medicine—treating the whole person instead of just specific medical problems.

This unrest led to the resignations and firings at La Paz of the chief lawyer, 4 board members, and 12 local leaders. Also, at the UFW convention in 1982 several staff members opposed Chavez by introducing their own candidates for office. Cesar Chavez's opponents even included his brother Richard, a son-in-law, and a sister-in-law. Chavez quickly fired them. However, this hurt union morale. Moreover, it led to a court case in which it was ruled that the firing of these people was unjustified. They had been properly elected union officials.

Gilbert Padillo had been with the UFW from the beginning and was forced into early retirement. "Cesar doesn't know how to delegate authority," Padillo said, "and became almost paranoid when others exercised some leadership."

In 1983, there was another setback for the UFW. The five-year agreements with the Teamsters ran out. Under those agreements, the UFW would organize the field-workers, and the Teamsters would organize the canners, packers, and farm truck drivers. The Teamsters gave no indication that they wanted their agreements to be renewed.

Also in 1983, the Republican governor of California, George Deukmejian, appointed people to the Agricultural Labor Relations Board who did not like unions for farm workers. They were defenders of the growers. This might be viewed as paying back a political debt. Agribusiness had contributed over $1 million to Deukmejian's campaign for governor. Almost all of the 1,000 union complaints against California growers were dismissed. What had happened to the ALRB was terribly disappointing to farm workers. "We thought we could redress our grievances through the Board, but it is not to be," said Cesar Chavez.

"Governor Deukmejian has literally destroyed the Agricultural Labor Relations Act," announced a saddened Chavez. "That act gave the workers the right to organize and bargain collectively. Without the law, we cannot organize unless we boycott. And that's why we are boycotting."

The grape boycott was on again in 1984. "We have more grievances in terms of pesticides, blacklisting, refusal to have fair and free elections with the grape growers than any other group of growers in California," said Chavez.

It sounded like the grape strike of the 1960s all over again. The UFW was still trying to get fair elections, good-faith bargaining with the growers, and testing for pesticide residues. Five pesticides in particular seemed to present the most health problems: captan, dinoseb, methyl bromide, parathion, and phosdrin. During the mid-1980s, 8 million pounds of pesticides were used annually in California. One-third of these pesticides are believed to cause cancer.

Farm workers are directly affected by pesticides. More than 300,000 farm workers were being poisoned a year in the United States in the mid-1980s. In fact, farm workers have the highest rate of worker-related injuries of any group of laborers in California. And the most dangerous crop of all to work with is grapes.

In 1985, Governor Deukmejian vetoed a bill requiring growers to post signs warning workers when fields have recently been sprayed with pesticides. The governor mentioned cost as a factor in his veto. But many questioned why the 14-billion-dollar-a-year agribusiness could not afford to post signs.

Pesticides are especially dangerous to children. There are high incidents of birth deformities and cancer among children of farm workers. This is true as well for children who live in towns near sprayed fields. One town particularly hard-hit was McFarland. This town of 6,000 near Delano is surrounded by vineyards regularly sprayed with pesticides. McFarland had 11 children stricken with cancer in a six-block area during a two-year period. (This is four times higher than the average for the area.) Six of them later died. Another town with a similar problem

109

Dolores Huerta and Linda Chavez (right) take part in a 1988 protest against the use of dangerous pesticides on table grapes.

was Fowler. This town of 3,000 had 7 children who had fallen ill with cancer.

Of the 300 million pounds of pesticides used to spray fields in California in 1984, only a small percentage reached the crops. Much of it drifted off into air or seeped into the water supply.

"We need to meet the growers and stop their madness at the marketplace," said Chavez. "If enough people join us and don't buy grapes, the growers will have to do something about the pesticides, at least in grapes. And once we get grapes, then we can go and get other products, too."

In 1985, Chavez tried to update the UFW by using computerized mailings to raise money. Just as the UFW farm worker was now making $5.15 an hour (the minimum rate allowed by law was much lower, $3.35 an hour), the union also had to stay in step with the times. Although the computer system cost $1.5 million, it was hoped the results would expand the $4 million UFW budget. Chavez also planned to use computers to help pinpoint stores for secondary boycotts. Then leaflets could be passed out to encourage people not to shop at stores that sell California table grapes. But the underlying reason for new techniques was that the old methods were out of date. There had been a change in people's attitudes. "Students won't join a picket line anymore," Chavez explained.

Even though times have changed, some of the other developments over the past few years sound almost like old news bulletins from the 1960s.

- On August 22, 1988, after 36 days, Cesar Chavez ended a water-only fast. The fast had been directed against the grape industry. Chavez was protesting the use of five particularly dangerous pesticides.
- On September 16, 1988, Dolores Huerta was badly hurt by police nightsticks. She was leading a protest against President George Bush's policies toward migrant farm workers on the President's visit to San Francisco.
- In 1989, the grape growers were still labeling Chavez a "terrorist" for his grape boycotts. Sometimes, the more things change, the more they remain the same.
- More reports began to come in about the long-range effects of chemicals. Claims were made that the town of Earlimart, California, was particularly in danger from cancers related to pesticides.
- On March 14, 1990, Cesar Chavez took part in a protest in Santa Monica, California, against the spraying of pesticides.
- On September 12, 1990, Chavez was arrested for protesting the use of pesticides on grapes outside a supermarket in Los Angeles.
- On October 10, 1991, Cesar Chavez took reporters on a tour of several citrus groves in the Coachella Valley to see the terrible living conditions of many field-workers. Paid as little as $2.50 an hour by labor contractors, these workers slept under trees (and had to pay $20 per month to do so),

111

drank water from irrigation pipes, and bathed in ditch water. "The conditions are what they were 30 years ago," said Cesar Chavez.

- In April 1992, Vons Companies supermarkets (one of the biggest buyers of California table grapes in southern California) stopped advertising grapes because of pressure from Chavez and the UFW. Shortly afterward, Vons began promoting their grapes again after receiving pressure from the California Table Grape Association.

In 1987, Chavez demanded a ban against five pesticides, claiming they cause birth defects, cancer, and other illnesses.

Perhaps it was in the area of preserving the environment that Cesar Chavez most keenly made his presence felt. Newspapers are filled daily with reports about the lowering of environmental quality. Some scientists say that we are in the grip of global warming. Others warn of the considerable damage being done to the ozone layer above the earth. Every week more species become extinct—creatures and plants that will exist only in memories and some day only in books. Other species are disappearing even before they can be discovered and named.

Cesar Chavez helped raise people's awareness about the health hazards of pesticides. Pesticides were once viewed as the miracle of the farmer. By controlling insects, farmers have been able to raise more crops. Now pesticides can be viewed as a ticking time bomb. And it is not only the farm workers who may be harmed. "These sprays are creepers," Chavez warned. "If they knocked you out immediately, it would be a lot easier to educate people and make our point."

Everyone should be concerned about the residue of chemicals left on the fruits and vegetables. One-third of the 8 million pounds of pesticides used annually in California may cause cancer. Chemicals also seep into the soil and then into the water supply. Chemical poisoning may even cause pregnant mothers to have children with birth defects.

In addition to his role as a protector of the environment, Cesar Chavez continued to provide leadership for the United Farm Workers. Even though in the 1990s Chavez was not doing as much field-by-field organizing, as much ranch-by-ranch picketing, he remained a frequent speaker, especially on college campuses. In 1992, Chavez even traveled as far away as Hong Kong, Singapore, and Taiwan to stress the importance of the boycott of California table grapes as a means of improving working conditions for the farm worker. Although the membership of the UFW may have shrunk in recent years, La Paz remains a center of education for farm worker issues.

"Most of them didn't know what a boycott was," once remarked Chavez, when talking about the awareness of both farm workers and average people in the 1960s of La Causa. "Things have changed a lot since then. We have first-, second-

and third-generation boycotters now. Boycotting grapes is Americano now."

In April 1993, Cesar Chavez returned to the area near Yuma where he had been born 66 years earlier. He was in San Luis, Arizona, to testify in the retrial of a lawsuit that had been brought by Bruce Church, Inc., against the United Farm Workers. (In 1988, this farm company had won a $5.4 million award against the UFW because of the union's boycott.)

On the evening of April 22, Chavez, who had recently ended a seven-day fast, was the houseguest at the home of a union supporter. After doing yoga exercises, Chavez complained of feeling tired and retired for the night. The next morning his body was discovered. Fully clothed, Chavez had died sitting in a chair, reading a magazine about Native American artifacts.

Immediately, the tributes began pouring in.

Art Torres, a California state senator and well-known Chicano politician, said: "He was our Gandhi. He was our Dr. Martin Luther King. It's hard to find people like him who epitomized the spiritual and political goals of a people."

Representative Jose Serrano, chair of the Congressional Hispanic Caucus called Chavez "an idol to all of us who believed in the value of unions and the idea of brotherhood."

Jerry Brown, the former governor of California, said Chavez was "probably the most important labor leader since World War II. He wanted to give power to the powerless. I believe that the movement will continue, that his legacy will not disappear."

And Bill Clinton, the President of the United States, declared: "The labor movement and all Americans have lost a great leader with the death today of Cesar Chavez. We can be proud of his enormous accomplishments and in the dignity and comfort he brought to the lives of so many of our country's least powerful and most dispossessed workers. Cesar Chavez was an authentic hero to millions of people throughout the world."

Some of those who viewed Chavez as a hero were the farm workers in the fields that day. After hearing the news, they walked in silence to the UFW headquarters in Salinas Valley, where they wept and prayed under a large photograph of Cesar Chavez. Perhaps their feelings were expressed best by a labor leader in

Cesar Chavez continued to lead the United Farm Workers until his death in 1993.

New York City. "For us," Dennis Rivera said, "the maestro is gone."

"We know he is irreplaceable," said Dolores Huerta, a long-time friend and vice-president of the UFW, "but people are in place to continue the work of the union."

A few days later, a rosary service was held in Delano, followed by an all-night vigil. By midmorning the next day a crowd of 25,000 had gathered to march the four miles from the park in Delano where the union leader's fast had been broken in 1968 to the union's one-time headquarters at Forty Acres for the funeral mass. Among those gathered were Native Americans, Hispanics, and Anglos, celebrities, friends, and farm workers. Just as on the march to Sacramento in 1966, there was drumming and singing, red-and-black union flags, and Chavez in the middle of the throng. Only this time the union leader was in a simple pine coffin fashioned by his brother Richard—a coffin so heavy that the pallbearers could shoulder it for no more than three minutes at a time. Among those taking their turns were actors Robert Blake and Martin Sheen; former California Governor Jerry Brown; the Reverend Jesse Jackson; the United States trade representative, Mickey Kantor, and U.S. Representative Joseph Kennedy. Even in death, Chavez had a way of getting people involved.

Over the years the role of Cesar Chavez as an American troublemaker may have lessened in the public's mind. Still, like Mahatma Gandhi before him, Chavez had shown how "in a gentle way you can shake the world." And Cesar Chavez had continued to have important things to say to us about the future. "We want sufficient power to control our own destinies," Chavez had explained. "This is our struggle. It's a lifetime job. The work for social change and against social injustice is never ended."

Although Cesar Chavez had clearly pointed out the need of unions for farm workers, it is in the field of the environment that Chavez may have made his most lasting contribution. Cesar Chavez had helped plant the seed to carry on the struggle until "the fields are safe for farm workers, the environment is preserved for future generations, and our food is once again a source of nourishment and life."

| 1927 | Cesario ("Cesar") Estrada Chavez is born on March 31 on a small farm near Yuma, Arizona. Cesar is the oldest of Juana Estrada and Librado Chavez's five children. |

1927   Cesario ("Cesar") Estrada Chavez is born on March 31 on a small farm near Yuma, Arizona. Cesar is the oldest of Juana Estrada and Librado Chavez's five children.

1937   Librado Chavez, Cesar's father, loses the family farm. The Chavez family joins the migrant workers who "follow the crop."

1942   After attending more than 30 schools, Cesar Chavez graduates from eighth grade, his last year of formal schooling.

1944   Chavez joins the U.S. Navy.

1948   Chavez marries Helen Fabela.

1952-62   Chavez works for the Community Service Organization (CSO). He starts out as an organizer and eventually becomes executive director.

1962   Chavez establishes the National Farm Workers Association (NFWA).

1965   Chavez organizes California grape pickers in what becomes a five-year strike.

1966   Chavez leads a march from Delano to Sacramento, California. Focus of attention on the plight of grape pickers begins a nationwide consumer boycott of grapes. The National Farm Workers Association merges with AWOC to become the United Farm Workers Organizing Committee (UFWOC).

1968   Chavez fasts for 25 days.

1970   The boycott forces grape growers to sign UFWOC contracts. The grape boycott ends, and the lettuce boycott begins.

1972	The United Farm Workers Organizing Committee (UFWOC) changes its name to the United Farm Workers of America (UFW) and gets a national AFL-CIO coordinator.
1973	Chavez and 3,500 members are jailed after refusing to limit picketing. Chavez leads a new grape boycott against grape growers who refuse to renew contracts.
1975	Farm workers win the right in California to bargain collectively through their union.
1978	Chavez ends boycotts of lettuce and grapes.
1985	Chavez leads a UFW march for an increase in wages and better working conditions.
1988	Chavez ends his 36-day fast to publicize the UFW boycott of California grapes and to press for stronger protection against pesticides. Dolores Huerta is beaten by police in a UFW protest during a visit to San Francisco by President George Bush.
1990	Chavez is arrested outside a supermarket for protesting the use of pesticides on grapes.
1991	Chavez undertakes an extensive speaking tour of colleges to spread the word about the UFW's boycott of California table grapes.
1992	Chavez serves as Visiting Lecturer in Farm Labor History in California at the University of California at Santa Monica. Chavez travels to Taiwan, Singapore, and Hong Kong (the third largest buyer of California table grapes after New York City and Los Angeles) to tell about working conditions and the effects of pesticides on farm workers.
1993	Cesar Chavez dies on April 22 at San Luis, Arizona.

GLOSSARY

AWOC Agricultural Workers Organizing Committee

barrio A Spanish-speaking section in a city or town.

blacklist A list of people who are disapproved of or who are to be punished (such as by refusing them jobs).

boycott To join with others in refusing to purchase certain products or services or to have any dealings with a person, organization, or store. The purpose is to express disapproval or to force acceptance of certain demands. (The word boycott comes from the name of a 19th-century land agent in Ireland. Farmers joined together against Charles Boycott for his refusal to reduce their rents.)

bracero A Mexican farm worker admitted to the United States for seasonal contract labor.

campesino A farm worker of Latin American heritage.

Chicano An American of Mexican descent. In Mexico, *chicano* is a slang term for a clumsy person. However, during the 1960s, young Mexican Americans began to use the term to indicate pride in their heritage and culture.

collective bargaining Negotiations between an employer and union representatives, usually about wages, hours, and working conditions.

colonia Spanish term for a Mexican immigrant neighborhood.

credit union A cooperative association that makes loans to its members at low interest rates.

CSO Community Service Organization.

el cortito Short-handled hoe.

huelga Strike.

injunction A court order prohibiting someone from doing something, or ordering someone to undo some wrong or injury.

lobbyist Someone who conducts activities aimed at influencing public officials, especially lawmakers.

mass The central ceremony in the Roman Catholic Church.

migrant worker A person who moves regularly in order to find work, especially in harvesting crops.

minimum wage The lowest legal wage that can be paid to a working person.

NFLU National Farm Labor Union.

NFWA National Farm Workers Association, the union Chavez began in 1962 for the grape pickers of California.

pachuco A young Mexican American who wore flashy clothes and belonged to a gang.

peregrinación Pilgrimage or march.

recall The right or procedure by which a public official may be removed from office before the end of his or her term of office by a special vote of the people.

scab A worker who takes the place of a striking worker.

secondary boycott The refusal to buy from, work for, or handle the products of an employer with whom a union has no dispute, with the purpose of forcing such an employer to stop doing business with an employer with whom the union does have a dispute.

sharecropper A farmer who works land for a landlord in return for a share of the crop.

Si, se puedes! Yes, you can! This was a cry that began in Arizona in 1974. It expressed optimism and determination.

sit-down strike A strike in which the workers stay in the place of work but refuse to work.

sit-in An act of sitting in the seats or on the floor of a business or organization as a means of organized protest.

stoop labor The work required when growing or harvesting a crop (such as a vegetable) that needs a lot of hand labor and bending.

strike The stopping of work by a group of workers in order to get the employer to agree to certain demands (such as improved working conditions, better wages, or changes in working hours).

strikebreaker A person hired to replace a striking worker.

subpoena A command to appear in court at a certain time and place to give testimony.

sweatshop A shop or factory where workers are employed for long hours at low wages and often under unhealthy working conditions.

sweetheart contract An agreement between an employer and a labor union in which special, favorable terms are given to one side or the other for the purpose of keeping a rival union out. The terms are often favorable to the employer and often arranged by a union official without the participation or approval of the union members.

UFW United Farm Workers of America.

UFWOC United Farm Workers Organizing Committee.

Viva la Causa! Long live the cause!

Viva la Raza! Long live the race, the people!

BIBLIOGRAPHY

and Recommended Readings

Day, Mark. *Forty Acres: Cesar Chavez and the Farm Workers.* New York: Praeger Publishers, 1971.

Dunne, John Gregory. *Delano: The Story of the California Grape Strike.* New York: Farrar, Straus & Giroux, 1967.

Fodall, Beverly. *Cesar Chavez and the United Farm Workers: A Selective Bibliography.* Detroit: Wayne State University Press, 1974.

*Franchera, Ruth. *Cesar Chavez.* New York: Harper & Row, 1970.

*Goodwin, David. *Cesar Chavez: Hope for the People.* New York: Ballantine Books, 1991.

Levy, Jacques. *Cesar Chavez: Autobiography of La Causa.* New York: W. W. Norton, 1975.

London, Joan, and Henry Anderson. *So Shall Ye Reap: The Story of Cesar Chavez & the Farm Workers' Movement.* New York: Thomas Y. Crowell Company, 1970.

Matthiessen, Peter. *Sal Si Puedes: Cesar Chavez and the New American Revolution.* New York: Dell Publishing Company, 1969.

Pitrone, Jean Maddern. *Chavez: Man of the Migrants.* Staten Island, N.Y.: Alba House, 1971.

*Roberts, Naurice. *Cesar Chavez and La Causa.* Chicago Childrens Press, 1986.

*Rodriguez, Consuelo. *Cesar Chavez.* New York: Chelsea House, 1991.

Taylor, Ronald B. *Chavez and the Farm Workers.* Boston: Beacon Press, 1975.

*Terzian, James P. and Kathryn Cramer. *Mighty Hard Road: The Story of Cesar Chavez.* Garden City, N.Y.: Doubleday, 1970.

*White, Florence Meiman. *Cesar Chavez: Man of Courage.* Champaign, Ill.: Garrard Publishing Co., 1973.

Yinger, Winthrop. *Cesar Chavez: The Rhetoric of Nonviolence.* Hicksville, N.Y.: Exposition Press, 1975.

*Young, Jan. *The Migrant Workers and Cesar Chavez.* New York: Julian Messner, 1972.

*Especially recommended for younger readers.

PLACES TO VISIT

Delano, California	• The house that served as Chavez's original headquarters for his union organizing.
Keene, California	• La Paz. The United Farm Workers headquarters and administration center. This is a community where people live and work. Tours can be arranged.

124

Burnham Holmes has written ten books for young adults. His most recent titles are *George Eastman* for the *Pioneers in Change* series and *The Third Amendment* and *The Fifth Amendment* for *The American Heritage History of the Bill of Rights* series.

Holmes teaches writing at the School of Visual Arts in New York City. Burnham, Vicki, and their son, Ken, live in New York City and near a lake in Vermont.

James P. Shenton is Professor of History at Columbia University. He has taught American History since 1951. Among his publications are *Robert John Walker, a Politician from Jackson to Lincoln; An Historian's History of the United States;* and *The Melting Pot.* Professor Shenton is a consultant to the National Endowment for the Humanities and has received the Mark Van Doren and Society of Columbia Graduates' Great Teachers Awards. He also serves as a consultant for CBS, NBC, ABC educational programs.

COVER ILLUSTRATION

Gary McElhaney

MAPS

Go Media, Inc.

PHOTOGRAPHY CREDITS

p.6 © Alan Pogue/Black Star; p.11 Archives of Labor & Urban Affairs, Wayne State University; p.14 AP/Wide World; p.18 AP/Wide World; p.22 Library of Congress; p.25 Library of Congress; p.27 Library of Congress; p.29 Archives of Labor & Urban Affairs, Wayne State University; p.31 Library of Congress; p.37 Library of Congress; p.41 UPI/Bettmann; p.43 AP/Wide World; p.46 Archives of Labor & Urban Affairs, Wayne State University; p.50 Archives of Labor & Urban Affairs, Wayne State University; p.52 Library of Congress; p.54 © Paul Fusco/Magnum; p.57 Library of Congress; p.59 Library of Congress; p.60 Archives of Labor & Urban Affairs, Wayne State University; p.64 AP/Wide World; p.67 AP/Wide World; p.70 AP/Wide World; p.77 Library of Congress; p.80 © Gene Daniels/Black Star; p.85 AP/Wide World; p.88 Library of Congress; p.90 UPI/Bettmann; p.96 AP/Wide World; p.101 AP/Wide World; p.107 UPI/Bettmann; p.110 AP/Wide World; p.111 UPI/Bettmann; p.113 UPI/Bettmann; p.115 UPI/Bettmann.